The Dynamics of Effective Prayer

By

Alistair Cole

Presenting a Biblical Theology of Prayer

Blessed is the one who reads the words of this prophecy, and blessed are those who hear it and take to heart what is written in it, because the time is near.
Revelation 1:3

Life Publications

Acknowledgements

Without the help and encouragement of the following, this book would never have been written. My wife, Lesley, and my daughters Nicola and Helen who spent many hours typing the manuscript.

To Carl Brettle for his counsel and advice in undertaking this task.

To my colleagues on the National Prayer Network Team of the Elim Pentecostal Churches.

To the great army of prayer partners that constitute the National Prayer Network of the Elim Churches.

To fellow prayer leaders of the Prayer Forum of the British Isles and Ireland.

To the team at the World Prayer Centre, Birmingham, England.

To David and Jan Holdaway for their advice in the presentation of the manuscript.

Thanks also to

Dr. R T Kendall, Rev. John Glass, Rev. Colin Dye, Rev. Lyndon Bowring, Jane Holloway and Ian Cole.

Dedication

This book is dedicated to my late parents, Edward (Ted) and Sally Cole, who were an inspiration to me; my wife Lesley and children Paul, Nicola and Helen because without their help and assistance, this book would not have been written; and to the leadership and congregation of the Elim Church, Glossop, Derbyshire.

Cover design by Graham Alder

Contact / E-mail alistair.l.cole@btinternet.com

CHAPTER SUMMARY

Moses would not undertake any leadership task without the assurance of God's presence. The prayer of Moses was a cry from the heart for God to be merciful to His rebellious people and for His presence to be manifest in their midst.

The greatest need of the church today is for there to be an awareness of the manifest presence of God in her life and ministry.

The intercessory prayer of Elijah became the conduit through which the power and glory of God was witnessed by the deranged Prophets of Baal. Passionate and prevailing prayer will be the means by which the power of God will be evidenced in the lives of believers and in the life and witness of the church.

There are times in which we are called upon to persist and persevere in prayer. Incidents from the lives of Abraham and Jacob clearly illustrate this important principle.

Forgiveness is at the heart of the Christian gospel and is granted in response to humble prayer. This is illustrated in God's dealings with David as he cried for mercy following his adultery with Bathsheba. God will always hear the cry of the penitent.

There is a powerful link between prayer and the prophetic and this is clearly seen in parts of the church that are currently experiencing renewal. This chapter examines instances in the lives of Solomon, Jehoshaphat, Hezekiah, and Daniel where prayer and the prophetic linked together to demonstrate God's power in the face of great danger.

Jesus said, *"When you pray."* This chapter examines the framework of prayer taught by Jesus to His disciples; a prayer commonly known as, *"The Lord's Prayer."*

The "High Priestly" prayer of Jesus recorded by John in the 17th chapter of his gospel reveals the intimacy that Jesus had with His Father as He prays firstly for Himself, for His disciples, and then for the church. A prayer prayed by Jesus just hours prior to the cross.

Jesus taught that, *"Men ought always to pray and not to lose heart."* This chapter deals with the importance of pressing through in prayer and seeing God respond to the heart cry of His people.

Jesus said, *"I will pray the Father and He will give you another helper!"* Jesus promised His disciples the mighty enabling power of the Holy Spirit as they embarked upon their mission of preaching the gospel. This chapter illustrates the link that exists between prayer and the outpouring of the Holy Spirit.

Following the events of the Day of Pentecost, the church was commissioned to preach the gospel to "All Nations." Prayer became the dynamic through which strategy for mission was established. A blueprint that holds true for the church of the 21st century.

The Christian life is a life of growth and fruit bearing. The Apostle Paul prayed earnestly for believers that they might grow in grace and experience the continuous anointing of the Holy Spirit. This chapter analyses the prayers of Paul recorded in his letter to the Ephesians.

The church is called upon to engage in high-level spiritual warfare. This will call for seasons of fasting as the believer seeks God for victory over the strategy of enemy forces.

The Dynamics of Effective Prayer

The Purpose of this Book

We are living during a period of momentous change in the spheres of politics, economics and the environment, to name but a few. This tide of change is sweeping through large sections of the church of Jesus Christ bringing renewal and a renewed passion for mission.

We are witnessing the most powerful mobilisation of prayer seen in the entire two thousand year history of the Christian church. This great movement of prayer is bearing fruit in transformed communities, cities, and in some cases, entire nations.

Recent global days of prayer have drawn together millions of believers spanning the continents and international time zones in a united cry for God to manifest His power and glory. This great initiative has been birthed through the vision of believers representing the nations of the African continent.

The purpose of this book is to present a Biblical framework for prayer in its varied expressions. Incidents from both the Old and New Testaments are examined to illustrate how prayer became the catalyst by which God's power was seen in the lives of nations and of individuals.

Prominent space is given to the vital role that prayer played in the life and ministry of Jesus. The entire direction and focus of His ministry was established as He came before His Father in prayer. Prayer also played a major role in the unfolding mission of the early church as the disciples sought to take the message of the gospel to the far flung reaches of the Roman Empire. The prayer dynamic of the New Testament church is clearly identified in the two chapters that examine the link between prayer and the power of the Holy Spirit, and prayer as a strategy for mission.

The Dynamics of Effective Prayer will guide the reader on an exciting journey in rediscovering how God responds to the prayers of His people.

Alistair Cole

Chapter 1

Prayer and Presence

M any parts of the world are currently witnessing a powerful outpouring of the Holy Spirit with great numbers of people coming to faith in Christ. Current statistics are suggesting that in excess of 7,500 per hour are entering the Kingdom of God. This great harvest is being accompanied by the presence of supernatural signs and wonders as God demonstrates His power in response to the preaching of the gospel. It is also apparent that where such moves of God are in evidence, the growth of the church is often paralleled by severe persecution. Hundreds of believers are daily paying the ultimate price of martyrdom for the sake of the gospel.

We may well ask the question, "What is the principal dynamic behind this great move of God?" Church history from the Acts of the Apostles onwards documents times of refreshing when suddenly, in the midst of what may appear to be a time of barrenness, God intervenes in demonstration of "Kingdom Power."

There are two significant factors that come into play here, factors that are apparent in every major revival,

a)   An increased level of anointing and power upon the preaching of the gospel, and in particular the message of the cross and resurrection of Jesus.

b)   A marked increase in the level of prayer and intercession calling upon God to impact the church, and to renew her cutting edge, thus equipping the church to influence and change communities, cities and nations.

Today we are witnessing a mighty wave of global prayer as millions of believers from every church background and from many nations call upon God for the salvation of the lost. Recent global days of prayer have drawn together nearly 500,000,000 people from every continent, spanning all the international time zones. Football stadiums filled with thousands of people, along with small groups of two's and three's, have joined together to call upon God to manifest His power among the nations. This great movement of prayer is catching the attention of world leaders as they grapple with the insurmountable problems that beset nations and communities.

Reports are to hand of incredible transformation taking place in nations, cities and communities. Major crime syndicates are being broken in response to powerful prayer initiatives. Reports of crime rates in towns and cities are falling with the police and law enforcement agencies acknowledging the part played by strategic prayer undertaken by groups of believers. The prayer movement is capturing the imagination of thousands of young people as they engage in initiatives such as 24/7. This has served to bring a radical cutting edge to the prayer life of the local church. There is also the increasing recognition among church leaders concerning the vital link between prayer and mission. It is futile to attempt any major evangelistic thrust without it being saturated with powerful and sustained prayer.

This great wave of prayer must also be understood as a major force in the great end time outpouring of the Holy Spirit which will usher in the return of Jesus Christ. The Old Testament prophet Joel makes mention of this sovereign move of God, his words were referred to by Peter as he preached on the Day of Pentecost,

> *And it shall come to pass afterward that I shall pour out of my Spirit on all flesh; your sons and your daughters shall prophesy, your old men shall dream dreams, your young men shall see visions. And on my menservants and on my maidservants I will pour out of my Spirit in those days.*
> Joel 2:28-29 (N.K.J.V)

So Why a Theology of Prayer?

The Bible teaches extensively on the subject of prayer. It is the principle means through which we are drawn into the presence of God. As we peruse the pages of the Old Testament, we see how that patriarchs, prophets, priests and kings engaged in prayer prior to making major decisions or going into battle. Jesus clearly taught the vital importance of prayer. Three times in Matthew 6 we read of Jesus acknowledging the importance of prayer,

"When you pray..."

Prayer played a major role in the life and ministry of Jesus:

Mark 1:35   **Early day**

> *And in the morning, rising up a great while before day, He went out, and departed into a solitary place, and there prayed.*

Luke 5:15-16 Following times of ministry

And great multitudes came together to hear, and to be healed of their sicknesses. And He withdrew Himself into the wilderness, and prayed.

Luke 6:12   Appointing His disciples

He continued all night in prayer to God.

(N.K.J.V)

What is the Greatest need in the Church today?

If this question were to be asked of a random group of people, the response would be varied. Some would argue that there needs to be a greater clarity and conviction in the preaching and teaching of scripture. Others would argue strongly for there to be a greater move towards more contemporary and culturally relevant forms of worship that can relate to this present generation. Others would advocate a much greater commitment towards evangelism and mission, to get out there and to bring in the harvest. There would be those who would argue for a community transformation and for the local church to be more involved in what is known as "Friendship Evangelism" There would be those who would see a priority being the response of the church to issues relative to the environment etc. It must be stressed that *all* of those issues are important and should find expression in every community of the saints. However, there is one factor that transcends all of these, one that is sadly lacking in much of the church scene, and that is the realisation of the manifest presence of God.

Where there is a sense of the presence of God, coupled with a high regard for His Person and Name, a floodtide of evangelism, worship, social action, dynamic preaching, soul winning and discipleship will break forth.

The church must of necessity recapture a sense of the awesome majesty of God. In many places this is beginning to happen, and we are seeing this in response to seasons of prayer in which there is a sense of barrenness, not only in the church, but also in the hearts of individuals. It is not unknown for prayer gatherings today to be punctuated by spontaneous expressions of wailing and lamenting as those gathered allow God to melt their hearts in response to the need of the moment.

Prayer and Presence – Moses

Moses was a leader who clearly understood that nothing could be accomplished without the manifest presence of God. Without God's presence the children of Israel would fail to inherit the Promised Land and would probably remain in Egypt as slaves.

In the book of Genesis we read of specific covenants that God entered into with Abraham, Isaac and Jacob. God promised each of these men that their seed would inherit a land of promise and that this would take the form of an "everlasting possession."

Genesis 17:8 **Promise to Abram (Abraham)**

> *I will give you and your descendants the land in which you are a stranger, all the land of Canaan, as an everlasting possession; and I will be their God.* (N.K.J.V)

God informed Abram (Abraham) that his descendants would be strangers in a land (Egypt) for 400 years, and that through God's mighty deliverance they would be freed and come out with great possessions.

Moses – The Burning Bush
Exodus 3

Moses had spent 40 years in the desert tending the flock of his father-in-law; Jethro. There would be much by way of routine in the everyday life of Moses as he sought to earn a living in what appeared to be a hostile desert environment. Suddenly things were about to change for Moses. What began as just another day was transformed by the presence of the Angel of the Lord as he spoke to Moses from the midst of a burning bush. A burning bush in a hot and arid desert would not have been an uncommon sight, but there was something different about this bush,

> *The bush burned with fire, but the bush was not consumed.*
>
> Exodus 3:2 (N.K.J.V)

Moses was suddenly confronted by the glory of God's presence. He was instructed to remove his sandals as he was standing on holy ground. This experience in the presence of God served to be the means by which the life of Moses would never be the same again. It was time to forsake a regular income and to launch out in faith in obedience to the will of God! Moses was to be God's chosen leader to lead His people out from under the slavery and yoke of the cruel Egyptians. God was mindful of the "covenants" He had entered into with Abraham, Isaac and Jacob, and now was the time for Him to act in accordance with His word.

Although Moses was initially reluctant to assume this role, he found himself before Pharaoh, requesting that freedom be granted to the children of Israel. There follows a series of protracted encounters between Moses and Pharaoh in which Pharaoh determines to block any attempt at freedom for God's people. Such was his determination, he imposed greater burdens on the people requiring them to work even harder. These delays, and Pharaoh's reluctance, caused the faith of Moses to be tested as he struggled to maintain credibility in the eyes of the officers of the children of Israel. Moses had to struggle with the accusations of failure and it caused him to cry to God in prayer,

> *Why have you brought trouble on this people? Why is it you have sent me? For since I came to Pharaoh in Your name he has done evil to this people, neither have you delivered your people at all.*
>
> Exodus 5:22-23 (N.K.J.V)

In the midst of this great test of faith, surrounded by serious personal doubt, Moses would often witness the awesome presence of God. As a result of Pharaoh's refusal to let the children of Israel go, the land of Egypt witnessed severe acts of the judgment of God. This would be in the form of devastating plagues that would decimate the infrastructure and economy of the nation.

The most dramatic manifestation of this judgement was soon to follow, and would come in the form of the death of the firstborn of the Egyptians. Moses and the people were to prepare for imminent freedom.

Each household of the children of Israel were to prepare a lamb, a male of the first year, without blemish, to sacrifice it and to apply its blood to the doorposts of their houses. God was to pass through the land of Egypt during the night in an awesome demonstration of His judgement resulting in the death of the firstborn of the land. In the midst of this God made a promise to Moses and the people,

> *And when I see the blood, I will Passover you; and the plague shall not be on you to destroy you when I strike the land of Egypt.*
>
> Exodus 12 :13 (N.K.J.V)

There follows the glorious scene of the exodus from Egypt as Moses leads the people out from the bondage of slavery. Pharaoh, in a moment of madness, changes his mind and sends for his best chariots to chase after the children of Israel to force them to return. When the Israelites saw the advancing hordes of the Egyptian army, and saw that they were hemmed in by mountains on each side and the sea ahead of them, they panicked and turned on Moses blaming him for leading them to what appeared certain destruction.

God once again demonstrated His mighty power by causing the people to "stand still" so they would see His glory as the waters of the sea divided allowing them to cross on dry land. They saw a further demonstration of the power of God as He caused the waters to turn back bringing total destruction to the armies of Egypt.

Moses and the people clearly saw the manifestation
of God's presence in the form of the plagues, the
Passover, the Exodus, and the destruction of
Pharaoh's armies!

The Giving of the Law
Exodus 19-20

Three months had elapsed since their deliverance from Egypt, three months in which the children of Israel had witnessed on several occasions the glory of God's provision. They had been led by the pillar of cloud by day and by the pillar of fire by night. God had miraculously provided them with daily food in the form of manna. He also provided them with water as they found themselves in a wilderness location with no obvious supply. The stage was now set for one of the most glorious manifestations of the power and presence of God recorded in scripture.

God called Moses to Sinai for the express purpose of giving him the commandments and precepts that if adhered to would guarantee them His blessing and prosperity in the land that they were about to inherit. God was calling His people to serve Him as a kingdom of priests and as a holy nation. They were to be to Him as a "special treasure" above all the people of the earth!

The initial response of the people was,

> ...all that the Lord has spoken we will do...
> Exodus19:8

God gave Moses specific instructions stipulating that clear boundaries were to be established at the base of Mount Sinai. No one should approach the mountain or in any way touch it on the pain of death. The people were to prepare to receive the law by washing themselves and by abstaining from sexual relations. The presence of God was manifested in thundering and lightnings with a thick cloud covering the top of the mountain. All of the people trembled before God, and the priests were to consecrate themselves before the Lord.

The Giving of the Law
Exodus 20

God announced Himself as the God who brought the people out of the land of Egypt and out of the house of bondage. There then followed the giving of the ten commandments, three of which have particular bearing upon the events recorded in chapters 32 and 33 of Exodus.

The Worship of other gods
Exodus 20:3-5

> You shall have no other gods before me. You shall not make yourselves a carved image, any likeness of anything that is in heaven above, or that is in the earth beneath, or that is in the water under the earth; You shall not bow down to them nor serve them... (N.K.J.V)

God was making it abundantly clear that under no circumstances would He tolerate the worship of any other god other than Himself! This was foundational to the ongoing relationship between God and His people, and their inheritance of the Promised Land was conditional upon their obedience to these commands. It is interesting to note that the standards required of God's people today are no less strict than the commands given in the days of Moses. God will not bring blessing and power to the church where there is complacency with regard to what may be termed "gods and idols."

The Golden Calf Incident
Exodus 32

The incident, which we have recorded in this chapter, serves to cast a shadow over God's dealings with His people. There was a delay in Moses returning from the mountain, this delay was interpreted by the people as Moses departing and leaving them bereft of leadership. The people respond by taking things into their own hands, and this, coupled with weak leadership on the part of Aaron, brings about a situation that had the potential for absolute ruin.

Aaron instructs the people to break off their golden earrings which he in turn fashioned with an engraving tool thus producing a model of a golden calf. The golden calf was a symbol of the Egyptian god "Amon" a god that was worshipped by the Egyptians as a sun god. God's mighty deliverance from the bondage of Egypt was soon forgotten as the people debauched themselves before this idol. The conduct of Aaron was lamentable in that he, too, was caught up in the rebellion of the people,

> *This is your God, O Israel, that brought you out of the land of Egypt...and Aaron made a proclamation and said, tomorrow is a feast to the Lord.*
>
> Exodus 32:4,5 (N.K.J.V)

The gods of Egypt

Animal worship was a major factor in the religious life of Egyptians. Such acts entailed gross sexual perversion causing the worshippers at times to completely lose control of themselves. This grave error was compounded by the fact that the golden calf became in reality "a substitute god," a "god" that would enable them to fulfill their most basic desires.

This incident has serious implications for the church today as she seeks to maintain her witness in an increasingly fragmented society. We live in an environment of "pluralism," the worship of many gods, and this has taken its toll upon the life and testimony of the church. Such practices only serve to erode any semblance of the presence of God, and is a principle factor behind the malaise that grips so much of Christendom today.

> When a person moves away from the biblical
> revelation of God, they end up with a religion
> that is a perversion.

The wrath of God was incurred as He witnessed the rebellion of the people. Such was His anger, He announced to Moses His intention to totally destroy the people on account of their sin!

This reaction by God to the sin of His people in the days of Moses should serve to remind us that today God still looks upon sin in the lives of His people as something that undermines His continued presence, and robs them of His blessing.

Moses the Intercessor

When God made His intention known to Moses, the heart of Moses was filled with sadness and despair. Moses takes it upon himself to plead before God on behalf of the people. In this passage we have one of the most powerful prayers of intercession recorded in scripture, and it is a prayer that serves as a "model" prayer to all those who engage in intercession,

Then Moses pleaded with the Lord his God, and said; Lord, why does your wrath burn hot against your people whom you have brought out of the land of Egypt with great power and with a mighty hand? Why should the Egyptians speak and say, He brought them out to harm them, to kill them in the mountains, and to consume them from the face of the earth? Turn from your fierce wrath and relent from this harm to your people.

Exodus 32:11-12 (N.K.J.V)

What are the Components of this Prayer?

A.   Moses pleaded. (Strenuous Prayer)

B.   These are YOUR PEOPLE whom you have redeemed from bondage.

C.   What about YOUR TESTIMONY before the Egyptians?

D.   Others will interpret this as YOUR FAILURE to bring YOUR PEOPLE into the land promised to Abraham, Isaac and Jacob!

This prayer of Moses was prayed with such intensity and passion that it moved the heart of God causing Him to respond.

God's Response

So the Lord relented from the harm which He said He would do to His people.

Exodus 32:14

What Lessons can we learn from the Prayer of Moses?

The church today is faced with monumental challenges to her witness and testimony. These challenges come from within and without. Such opposition calls for believers to engage in the level of praying entered into by Moses. This need is most apparent in the life of the church in the West.

The church in the West today resembles the conditions prevailing in the church at Ephesus recorded for us in the second chapter of Revelation.

A Warning

> *Nevertheless I have this against you, that you have left your first love, remember therefore from where you have fallen; repent and do the first works, or else I will come unto you quickly and remove your lamp stand from its place...*
>
> Revelation 2:3-5 (N.K.J.V)

History records how the church in Ephesus, along with the other six churches mentioned in Revelation, closed as the presence of God gradually lifted from their life and witness.

The prophet Habakkuk found himself in such a situation as he contemplated the coming judgement of God upon the nation of Judah, his prayer was clear,

> *Lord, I stand in awe of your fame; I stand in awe of your deeds oh Lord. Renew them in our day, in our time make them known; in wrath remember mercy.*
>
> Habakkuk 3:2 (N.I.V)

Prayer and Presence
Exodus 33

God had relented from His threat to destroy the children of Israel on account of their rebellion. We now see the story move a stage further where again we see Moses pleading before God for Him to manifest His divine presence.

God announces to Moses that He would send an angel to accompany the people on their journey to the Promised Land,

> *For I will not go up in your midst, lest I consume*
> *you on the way, for you are a stubborn people.*
> Exodus 33:3 (N.K.J.V)

In response to this, Moses took his tent and pitched it outside the camp and called it; "The Tabernacle of Meeting." In this tent Moses would commune with God and there he would speak to God face to face as a man would speak to his friend. Those who witnessed this could see the glory of God's presence at the door of the tent. For Moses, the thought of undertaking this great journey in his own strength was a prospect that caused him great distress. There was one thing that Moses desired more than any other and this was the assurance that God was with him.

The Heart Cry of Moses

> *Then Moses said to Him, if Your presence does not*
> *go with us, do not bring us up from here.*
>
> Exodus 33:15

How will it be known, cried Moses, that your people and I have found grace in your sight except you go with us? Moses was not concerned as to his status as a successful leader, at this point in time he had no regard for his own reputation. Moses heart was for God's people to realise their promised inheritance, and that through it God's great Name might be magnified.

God's Response to the Heart of Moses

> *So the Lord said to Moses, I will also do this thing that you have spoken; for you have found grace in my sight, and I know you by name.*

Exodus 33:17

Conclusion / Prayer and Presence

Much can be learned from this incident of the golden calf. Aaron and the people were guilty of taking their eyes off God and in doing so sought to move forward in their own strength and through their own ideas. They failed to realise that their actions would cost them the presence and protection of God.

This is a situation that sadly is apparent in much of church life today. We live in the age of "the consumer church," this approach conditions people to think in terms of "what can this church do for me?" This serves to erode any understanding of the vital importance of discipleship and service. Anointed, Spirit filled leadership can be usurped by what may appear to be a "media driven" dimension, causing people to be drawn by the groups which produce the most glitzy advertising and promotional campaign. Much of this is an offence to Almighty God and causes the lifting of His presence.

Conditions such as these must bring God's people to their senses. Without the presence of God we are nothing, we are no better than the confused misguided children of Israel who sought to put their trust in a "substitute god." Failure and defeat quickly followed.

Moses clearly was a man of prayer, yet his abiding passion was to be in the presence of the living God, and his prayers strongly reflected this desire. The church today is thankfully re-discovering the power of prayer, and it must be the desire of every believer to experience for themselves the power and victory that comes with the abiding sense of God's presence.

A Final Prayer

> *Please, show me your glory.*
>
> Exodus 33:18

The Dynamics of Effective Prayer

Chapter 2

Prayer and Power

Having seen the vital importance of experiencing the presence of God through prayer we now move on a stage further to discover the part that prayer plays in the manifestation of His power.

That God is a God of awesome power is a fact that just cannot be denied. The pages of scripture abound with references to the power of God at work in so many ways. We see His great power demonstrated at creation as He literally spoke the created order into being,

> *Then God said, let there be light; and there was*
> *light.*
> Genesis 1:3:(N.K.J.V)

This first chapter of Genesis has numerous references to the power of God's spoken word, and this theme is mentioned in many other parts of scripture. The writer to the Hebrews reminds us that God upholds all things by the word of His power. Careful study of the Old Testament books will convince the reader of the awesome and limitless scope of the power of God. The story of

29

His dealings with His people Israel contains many instances in which His power was manifested both in times of need and in times of victory.

As we examine the gospels we see portrayed vivid accounts of the power and authority of Jesus as He taught and demonstrated the Kingdom of God. Luke makes reference to the words spoken by the prophet Isaiah as he foretold the nature of Christ's ministry. It would be a ministry that would reach out to meet the needs of the poor, the broken-hearted, the captives, the blind, and the oppressed. Jesus demonstrated this authority in response to the anointing of the Holy Spirit that was upon Him. The New Testament narrative continues as we see the Holy Spirit poured out upon the disciples and the early church, enabling them to replicate the ministry of Jesus in true apostolic power.

The Challenge to the Church

The church has been equipped to declare this great message of the gospel of the kingdom not in her own power but in the power of the Holy Spirit. The church is facing an onslaught from enemy forces bent upon restricting her message and witness. Laws are in the process of being framed that will curb the freedom of preachers to speak in terms of Jesus being the only means of access to God. Preaching of this nature would be considered offensive to those of other faiths. The battle lines are drawn, and it is a battle that cannot be fought on the grounds of logic or persuasion. The church is being called upon to cry to God as Elijah did on Mount Carmel, calling upon Him to "send the fire,"

And the God who answers by fire, He is God.
1 Kings.18:24 (N.K.J.V)

Religious orthodoxy and practice has failed a generation particularly in the West. The man in the street has looked at the church and has concluded that her message is one of confusion, lacking in relevance, and one that fails to address real life issues. This sadness is magnified as we compare this present situation to the vibrancy that was the hallmark of Christ's ministry and that of the apostles and the early church. The preaching of the Kingdom of God is a message that sweeps aside mere religion and replaces it with the transforming power of Jesus Christ.

The gospel writers record how Jesus openly rebuked the religious leaders of the day for their hypocrisy and failure to engage with the real needs of their society. In marked contrast to the religious system that prevailed, the common people gladly received Jesus and were inspired by His teaching and ministry. It was said of Jesus, *"Never man spoke like this man!"* Paul reminds us that the gospel is not a gospel of word only, but it is a gospel of power. The manifestation of this supernatural power was in direct response to the level of prayer entered into, firstly by Jesus, and subsequently the apostles and early church.

What should be the response of the Church today?

Whilst it is right for there to be a clear understanding of the nature of the battle faced by the church today, we must nevertheless constantly remind ourselves that in prayer we have the supreme weaponry at our disposal with which to engage the enemy.

> The time has come for the church to seek the face of God as a matter of great urgency. There must be a cry from the hearts of God's people for Him to demonstrate His power in and through the life and witness of the church!

Our motives need to be clear in this; we are not in the business of seeing who can build the largest church in town, we are not called to build "Church," we are called to build the kingdom. All over the world entire communities are experiencing spiritual transformation through the prayers of God's people. This transformation that is being carried along on the wing of prayer is not just a revival of religion, it is a sovereign visitation of God in which His power is clearly shown in changed lives and renewed churches.

What should our Prayer Focus be?

Our prayer focus should be for Jesus to once again take centre stage in the life of the church. This will require sustained levels of prayer and fasting as the people of God call upon Him to restore the cutting edge to the life and witness of the church, coupled with a restoration of the preaching of the cross and resurrection of the Lord Jesus Christ. There has been an alarming decline in the standard of preaching in much of the church today, and this is one of the principle reasons behind the decline of Christian witness and testimony. This was the secret of Paul's approach. He was an eminent theologian, he was a man of letters, and yet he realised that none of the great ability he possessed had the power to change lives,

> *For the message of the cross is foolishness to those who are perishing, but to us who are being saved it is the power of God.*
> 1 Corinthians 1:18 (N.K.J.V)

Paul's prayer for the church at Corinth was that their faith should not stand in the wisdom of men, but in the power of God.

Prayer and Power – Elijah
James 5, 1 Kings 17-18

The vital link between prayer and the manifestation of the power of God is clearly seen in and through the life and ministry of Elijah and in particular his confrontation with the prophets of Baal at Carmel.

The religious climate of Elijah's day bore a strong resemblance to the conditions the church finds herself in today. There had been a massive falling away from the worship of the Lord God of Israel, and a turning to the worship of pagan idols; namely the cult god Baal. This came to the fore following the rise of Ahab to the throne of Israel. Ahab's reign was one of repeated disaster and calamity for the nation. This zeal for idolatry, coupled with his fateful marriage to Jezebel, brought the wrath of God upon His people.

The events surrounding the reign of Ahab and the early ministry of Elijah contain some very pertinent lessons for us today as we seek to respond to the challenge facing us.

The nation of Israel, under the rule of King Ahab, was locked into a situation in which religious life was expressed through the worship of many gods. This led to the erosion of truth and a moving away from standards of righteousness and justice. This lurch toward the worship of foreign gods was to have disastrous consequences for the nation. We see the same pattern emerging today as nations give way to 21st century idols. The term "post Christian" is now an accepted term in Western society.

There are two central characters to this story, both men with strong convictions, and both convinced that they were the guardians of the truth.

King Ahab

Ahab was a man of contrasting abilities, he was an able and prosperous king, a soldier of consummate skill, but he allowed himself to be overwhelmed by the wickedness of idolatry,

> *Now Ahab the son of Omri did evil in the sight of the Lord, more than all who were before him.*
>
> 1 Kings 16:30 (N.K.J.V)

He lost all sense of righteousness and he considered his actions in leading the nation into idolatry as a mere "trivial thing." His greatest mistake was to enter into marriage with Jezebel, daughter of Ethbaal, King of the Sidonians, and it was through her evil influence that Ahab was led astray.

The conduct and character of Ahab is adequately described in the following verse,

> *And Ahab made a wooden image. Ahab did more to provoke the Lord God of Israel to anger then all the kings of Israel who were before him.*
>
> 1 Kings 18:33 (N.K.J.V)

His action was in clear violation of the first two commandments given to Moses at Sinai,

> *You shall have no other God's before me. You shall not make yourself a carved image - any likeness of anything that is in heaven above, or that is in the Earth beneath, or that is in the water under the earth.*
>
> Exodus 20:3-4

Any form of worship to such an idol was an act of direct rebellion against God and would incur His wrath and judgement!

Baal – "Master Possessor"

The meaning of his name adequately describes the danger involved in entering into any form of worship. Worship of Baal was the equivalent to what we understand today as the giving of one's self to the power of the occult. Such practice caused great destruction in Elijah's day and the same is true today.

Baal was originally a Phoenician god that became a snare to generations of Israelites. Worship of Baal was a prominent feature of the religious life of Canaan prior to the land being taken over by Joshua and the children of Israel. God had instructed Joshua and the people to go in and possess the land, and to purge the land from every form of idol and false god. Possession and security of the land would be conditional upon the people being obedient to this directive. Failure to do this would result in severe judgement and oppression by foreign powers. Drought, crop failure, famine, and pestilence would follow if the people of God ever chose to turn away from God to the worship of such idols!

Ahab failed to reflect upon instances in the history of the nation in which worship of Baal incurred the wrath and judgement of a holy and righteous God. The book of Judges records how following the conquest of Canaan, the Israelites forsook the Lord who had brought them into the Promised Land, and turned to the worship of Baal,

> *They forsook the Lord and served Baal and the Ashtoreths. And the Angel of the Lord was hot*

against Israel. So He delivered them into the hands of plunderers who attacked them; and He sold them into the hands of their enemies all around, so that they could no longer stand before their enemies.

Judges 2:13-14 (N.K.J.V)

This episode in the history of the nation should have acted as a clear warning to Ahab of the fearful consequences that would ensue if he continued in this way. The writer of the Judges vividly describes how due to this rebellion, Israel could not stand before her enemies. This, sadly, is a commentary upon much of the church of Jesus Christ in our day. Unconfessed and habitual sin has made such inroads into the vital fabric of the body of Christ that she now finds herself weak and bereft of power, and her testimony compromised!

This condition perhaps more then any other surely must be the reason for the urgency that is required on the part of God's people to humble themselves and repent, crying to God for spiritual renewal and power.

Baal: His alleged power base

Baal was revered as the god who controlled agriculture and was responsible for the germination and growth of crops. He was also the god who controlled the weather patterns and so could precipitate rainfall.

What did worship of Baal entail?

Worship of Baal would entail gross acts of sexual perversion and cult prostitution. Special poles were erected at strategic sites throughout the land, and around these poles would be the enactment of fertility rites often involving the sacrifice of children. This would be accompanied by the most hideous of occultic practises imaginable, which very often led to death.

Elijah: A Man for a Crisis

The other central character of this gripping story is the Prophet Elijah. The nation spiritually was at a low ebb, idolatry was rampant, and many of the prophets of the Lord had been butchered at the hands of Ahab's evil wife Jezebel. Suddenly into the narrative appears this remarkable man Elijah. He was an uncompromising character, and one who had grown up in the rugged geographical outposts of Jabesh-Gilead, the very last person that one would associate as being a prophet of God. Although we cannot fail to be impressed with the power and authority of this man, we must always remember that the scripture describes him as being a very ordinary man, one who experienced failure and defeat so soon after the confrontation on Mount Carmel,

> *The effective, fervent prayer of a righteous man avails much.* James 5:16 (speaking of Elijah)
> (N.K.J.V)

The Amplified Bible renders this verse so graphically, and in so doing draws our attention to the potential power of prayer, a power exercised by Elijah,

> *The earnest, heartfelt, continued prayer of a righteous man makes tremendous power available, and is dynamic in its working!*

These words should inspire and motivate us in our praying day by day. It is very easy to be taken up with the successes of Elijah, but James here reminds us that he was a man who experienced the same struggles and battles we face, he wrestled with the same idiosyncrasies, and this is something that must be borne in mind as we find ourselves engaged in prayer. We must never think of prayer as being the preserve of the so called "spiritually mature," those who have known the Lord for a long period of time. Whenever the enemy would seek to assail us with this notion of inadequacy, we can take heart in the knowledge that this great man of God, so powerfully used of God, also faced the same pressures that we face on a daily basis.

In spite of his humble background and rugged demeanour, Elijah was God's man for the hour of crisis. He was given the specific task of confronting King Ahab and announcing to him that on account of his sin, the judgement of God was about to come upon the nation,

> *As the Lord God of Israel lives before whom I stand, there shall not be dew nor rain these years, except at my word.*

1 Kings 17:1(Ahab confronted)   (N.K.J.V)

There are three important factors concerning the ministry of Elijah portrayed in this verse,

a)   His boldness: He came before the despotic King Ahab without any thought of his own safety.

b)   His authority: The source of his authority was the Lord God of Israel.

38

c)   His message: There shall not be dew nor rain, except at
       my word.

Ministry on this scale must of necessity be prefaced and
accompanied by strong intercessory prayer. As the events unfold
in this story we shall see this to be true.

Three years were to elapse before Elijah would be the conduit
through which the power of God would be manifested on Carmel.
However, there were foundations to be laid in the life and
experience of Elijah that would prepare him for that momentous
event. Elijah was at pains to point out that he was not on some
political or diplomatic mission, nor was he entering into
"negotiation" with Ahab. He was the servant of God, sent by
God, to pronounce judgement upon Ahab and the nation. This
pattern of ministry is one that is being replicated in many parts of
the church today and it is happening through the coming together
of these two great streams; "Prayer and the Prophetic." God is
raising up the Prophetic, people whose ministry is saturated by
the prayers of God's people. Such ministries are beginning to
impact nations at the highest level, and are an integral part of the
present day outpouring of the Holy Spirit taking place in many
parts of the world today.

God's Provision for Elijah

During this three year period in which there was no rain in the
land, Elijah experiences the supernatural provision and protection
of God in a most remarkable way. These events are recorded for
us in 1 Kings 17, a passage that should be mandatory reading for
all who may be passing through times in which their faith is being
tested! Elijah was to face the ultimate challenge to his walk with
God at Carmel, therefore his experiences recorded for us in this

great chapter were the means by which God was preparing him to face the prophets of Baal. If we are serious about being used for God in any way, and in particular the ministry of prayer and intercession, then we must be ready for such seasons of testing.

Elijah was instructed to turn eastward and hide by the brook Cherith,

> *I have commanded the ravens to feed you there!*
>
> 1 Kings17:4 (N.K.J.V)

We read here how Elijah went and did according to the Word of God staying by the brook. In an act of incredible provision, bearing in mind that there was a drought, God ordained that the ravens should bring Elijah food on a daily basis. This went on for a season, but eventually the brook dried up and it was time for Elijah to move on.

Zarephath – Elijah and the Widow

The word of the Lord came to him again directing him to Zarephath where he would meet a widow who would provide for him. Upon meeting the widow, it would seem to Elijah that he had embarked upon a futile task. Far from being in a position to feed the man of God, the widow was in the process of scraping together some meager rations for her and her son before they would both fall victim to the adverse conditions caused by the drought.

To ask this woman to prepare a meal for him in these circumstances was at the very least an unreasonable demand. The woman protested at the seeming lack of sensitivity on the part of Elijah, could he not see that she was in a position of total destitution? Then suddenly, in the midst of this confusion, the word of the Lord came from the lips of the prophet,

> *For thus says the Lord God of Israel: the bin of flour shall not be used up, nor shall the jar of oil run dry, until the day the Lord sends rain on the earth.*
>
> 1 Kings17:14 (N.K.J.V)

The spirit of faith that was upon Elijah elicited an immediate response from the woman in that she went and did according to the instruction of the Man of God. The result was that she, Elijah and her house did eat for many days.

The Widow's Son: Prayer and Power

The son of the widow woman was taken seriously ill resulting in his untimely death. The woman interpreted this as an act of God's judgement and that Elijah was acting as God's agent in bringing that judgement about. Elijah responded by taking the boy in his arms and carrying him to the upper room of the house where he laid him on his own bed. Elijah, with all the passion at his disposal, calls upon God to intervene in an act of mighty power,

> *Oh Lord my God, I pray, let this child's soul come back to him. Then the Lord heard the voice of Elijah; and the soul of the child came back to him, and he revived.*
>
> 1 Kings1:21-2 (N.K.J.V)

God demonstrated his power in response to the heart cry of Elijah. There is one part of this verse that tells us something that is universally true in respect of prayer; namely, that God hears us. Every cry from the heart, every sigh, every petition, all of these are heard by God and He responds to them in accordance with His will. Only the presence of unconfessed sin and willful disobedience will cause our prayers not to be heard by God,

> *If I regard iniquity in my heart, the Lord will not hear.*
>
> Psalm 66:18 (N.K.J.V)

These three instances in which Elijah proved and experienced the power of God had brought him to the place where he was now ready for the ultimate challenge.

The Challenge to Ahab

Elijah sends word to Ahab via his servant Obadiah,

> *Now therefore, send and gather all Israel to me on Mount Carmel.*
>
> 1 Kings 18:19

This was to be the prelude to one of the most dramatic manifestations of God's power recorded in scripture, and it happened in response to prayer. Elijah, one man, faced the combined challenge of the 450 prophets of Baal. Elijah openly challenged them to prove that Baal was the true god. It was time for them to make their minds up, they could no longer falter between two opinions!

The Nature of the Challenge

> *You call upon the name of your gods, and I will call upon the name of the Lord; and the God who answers by fire, let him be God.*
>
> 1 Kings 18:24

Here we have Elijah standing alone before these ardent prophets of Baal, laying down the gauntlet in an act of incredible faith and trust in the living God. As has been previously stated, this incident involving Elijah is a mirror image of the challenge facing the church today. Elijah's challenge was based on the manifestation of power; in other words let Baal prove that he is the one and only god by showing forth his power!

This verse should be a supreme motivation to every believer to engage in prayer for a breaking forth of God's power in and through the church. There is currently a huge offensive being mobilised by forces determined to capture the hearts particularly of the young. The spiritual life of the nation of Great Britain is at this point in time up for grabs, and the only way for the church to take back lost ground is for there to be a concerted cry to God for a demonstration of kingdom power.

Self-Mutilation

Elijah invites the prophets of Baal to cry to him to send the fire. For six hours they cry and scream for Baal to answer them but to no avail. They mutilate themselves, they cut themselves with knives and lances causing their blood to gush. Eventually, after six fruitless hours, Elijah calls a halt to the carnage and calls upon the prophets of Baal to come near to him.

Faith Energised by Prayer
Faith's Confidence

> *Then Elijah said to all the people, come near to me. So all the people came near to him. And he repaired the altar of the Lord that was broken down.*
>
> 1 Kings18:30

The first act of Elijah following the ranting of Baal's prophets was to rebuild the altar of the Lord that had been broken down. This spectacle of the broken down altar has clear implications for the church in our day. Elijah could not proceed without the rebuilt altar, the same is true for us today. A broken down altar speaks of a lack of prayer. One of the great deficiencies in the church today is the lack of emphasis given to prayer. It is a common thing for prayer to be pushed to the margins of the life of the local church, but it is equally true that denominational leaders so very often are guilty of placing prayer well down their list of priorities in relationship to national ministry. This is a deficiency that requires urgent attention if we are serious in our quest to win a nation for Jesus.

Elijah rebuilt the altar in the name of the Lord and in doing so took twelve stones, each representing one of the Tribes of Israel. Elijah, in taking these twelve stones, was preparing for national repentance. In our great regional and national prayer initiatives today we are doing the same, we are contending for the soul of the nation.

Faith's Conviction

Here we see Elijah drawing near to God in prevailing prayer,

44

Lord God of Abraham, Isaac, and Israel, let it be known this day that you are God in Israel, and that I am your servant, and that I have done these things at your word. Hear me O Lord, hear me, that this people may know that you are the Lord God, and that You have turned their hearts back to You again.

1 Kings18:30-37

A Model Prayer of Intercession

This prayer of Elijah's stands as a "model prayer" to those who engage in calling upon the Name of the Lord. Let us break down this prayer and examine its component parts.

"Lord God of Abraham, Isaac, and Israel" –

Elijah is praying to the God of history, to the God who has made covenants with His people.

"That you are God in Israel" –

That you are the "only" God.

"That I am Your Servant" –

Elijah was not involved in status seeking ministry. This approach is so diametrically different from the "consumer church" ethos we see in Christendom today.

"That I have done these things at Your Word" –

This was no mere exercise in religion, this was Elijah demonstrating total obedience to the Lord His God.

"That You have turned their hearts back to You" –

Not just who can have the biggest church in town, no, this was a cry from the heart of Elijah for national renewal and revival.

There is nothing of Elijah contained in this prayer, it was a cry from his heart for God to manifest his awesome power in response to the deranged prophets of Baal.

45

Faith's Conquest

> *Then the fire of the Lord fell and consumed the*
> *burnt sacrifice, and the wood and the stones and*
> *the dust, and licked up the water that was in the*
> *trench.*
>
> 1 Kings 18:38

God heard the prayer of Elijah, and in response to the idolatry and rebellion of Ahab and his henchmen, He sent the fire. The fire of God's glory reduced the altar and sacrifice to rubble. This demonstration of power had an immediate effect on the prophets of Baal,

> *Now when all the people saw it they fell on their*
> *faces; and they said, the Lord, He is God! The*
> *Lord, He is God!*
>
> 1 Kings 18:39

This persuasion did not come through the preaching of Elijah, it came through an awesome manifestation of the power of God given in response to his prayer!

The Sound of Abundance of Rain

Baal was supposedly the god who had control over the weather patterns and would therefore control rainfall. Elijah instructed Ahab to go up and prepare himself a meal for there was the sound of abundance of rain. Elijah then instructed his servant to go to the summit of Carmel whilst he prayed and once again sought the face of God. Six times Elijah's servant went to the summit but saw no evidence of changing weather patterns, but Elijah instructed him to go a seventh time,

*The seventh time he said, there is a cloud the size
of a man's hand, rising out of the sea!*

1 Kings 18:44

This tiny cloud silhouetted against the broad expanse of blue sky was the symbol of advancing rain. This was the time to prepare for the abundance of rain, the long years of drought were about to come to an end.

The Small Cloud – A Prophetic Symbol

The church in the West has passed through a long period of barrenness and dryness, but it would seem that God is beginning to stir the hearts of His people. The great prayer gatherings that are taking place, particularly those that are directly linked with mission, are what could be described as clouds the size of a man's hand. There is much to be done, there are momentous challenges still facing God's people, but He is responding to those who are crying to Him for Him to manifest His glory.

Let us conclude this chapter by reminding ourselves of the words written by the Apostle James when he describes the incredible power of prayer,

*The earnest, heartfelt, continued prayer of a
righteous man makes tremendous power available,
and is dynamic in its working!*

James 5:16 (Amplified Bible)

Chapter 3

Prayer and Persistence

"Persist" –
to continue firmly or obstinately
in a course of action

Persistence is a quality that can be used in both a positive and a negative way. When one is engaged in the pursuit of something that will be of help and assistance to another, such as raising much needed finance for a worthy cause, or seeking to be thorough in the completion of an assigned task, situations such as these call for persistence to be exercised in a positive manner. Persistence can also be expressed in negative ways. Persistent bad behaviour can be a cause of offence and distress to many. In recent years there has been a series of programmes on UK television channels entitled; *Neighbours From Hell.* These documentary programmes depict in graphic detail the distress experienced by people who find themselves victims of unruly and unreasonable neighbours who persist in unsocial behaviour. A child may need to be reprimanded if he or she persists in certain patterns of conduct. Those who persist in criminal activities will feel the full weight of the judicial system unless they mend their ways. A doctor may need to warn a patient that if they persist in a certain lifestyle, i.e. binge drinking, overeating, smoking etc., such persistence may eventually seriously damage their health.

When we use the term "persistence" in relation to prayer, we will soon discover that dramatic changes may occur in respect of the matter being prayed for. There is an urgent need both in the life of the individual believer, and in the corporate life of the church, for persistence in prayer. There is a danger that prayer can be entered into as an exercise of mere convenience, a practice that we resort to only in times of great crisis. When every other human instinct fails, and every effort we make to solve the problem comes to nothing, then there is the pushing of the panic button, and as a last resort, we pray! Suddenly God is prevailed upon to stop all that He is doing and attend to the situation we face. Now, we need to affirm that it is right that we call upon Him in those times of need, He is there to hear every heartcry and He will respond, but God desires a relationship of intimacy with His people, a relationship held together by communion and fellowship, and a prayer dynamic that is not mechanical, but one that flows from the heart.

The life and health of the local church will be determined by the level of prayer undertaken. There needs to be a radical change in the way in which prayer is expressed in our corporate prayer gatherings. So many church prayer meetings have become the preserve of the faithful few who pray in all sincerity, but sadly much of this prayer is not rooted in the real life issues that face people and communities. This is a pattern that needs to be broken, it is a far cry from the dynamic prayer life experienced by the early church. We have recorded in the book of Acts instances of buildings being shaken and prison doors being opened, and powerful miracles of healing, and multitudes coming to faith in Christ following seasons of persistent prayer. There was a determination in these prayer gatherings to persevere in prayer until God had clearly intervened in demonstration of His power.

It must not be thought that persistent prayer requires great physical exertion or energy. However, there will be times when we may be called upon to "wrestle" with God over a particular issue. There are many instances recorded in scripture where people literally had to devote hours in pressing through to God. Daniel, although faint and weak, prayed for three weeks before the answer came.

The prayer of Jesus in the garden of Gethsemane was so intense that it caused great sweat drops of blood to fall from His body.

How do we engage in Persistent Prayer?

The best place to start is to examine notable examples of such prayer recorded for us in scripture,

> *Men ought always to pray and not to lose heart.*
>
> Luke18:1 (N.K.J.V.)

> *They ought to always pray and not to turn coward, faint, lose heart and give up!*
>
> Amplified Bible

There is much talk in Christendom today concerning the need of renewal or as some would say "Revival" in the church particularly in the West. Sadly, much of this discussion is at best cosmetic. Renewal, revival, whatever term we choose to use, will only come as the people of God persist in prayer. God will always respond to fervent prayer flowing from the lips of His people, and in response to this will bring about change in the most extreme of circumstances. Great men and women of God dating back through the pages of the Bible can inspire us as we see how they engaged in persistent prayer in the face of daunting challenges to their faith.

Abraham – A Prayer of Intercession
Genesis 18

Here was a man who time and time again proved God in the midst of great adversity and trial. If ever a man was called upon to walk by faith it was Abraham. Coming from a wealthy background, accustomed to a comfortable standard of living, Abram, as he was initially known, heard the voice of God instructing him to forsake his comfort zone, to leave his own country and his father's house, and go by faith to a land that God would show him. This call was accompanied by a specific promise given to Abram assuring of God's blessing and provision in return for his obedience,

> *I will make you a great nation; I will bless you and make your name great; and you shall be a blessing. I will bless those who bless you, and I will curse him who curses you, and in you all the families of the earth shall be blessed.*

> Genesis 12:2 – 3 (N.K.J.V)

Abram immediately responded to the call of God, he took Sarai his wife, and Lot, his brother's son, and all of his possessions and departed for the land of Canaan.

This promise of God's blessing that would be upon Abram, and through him upon all families of the earth, was established in the form of a "covenant," it was a covenant specifically given to Abram.

The Abrahamic Covenant
God's Promise

a)   Abram would be the father of a great nation.

b)   God would bless him and make him great.

c)   All the families of the earth would be blessed through Abram.

The word that God spoke to Abram was specific; his descendants would be as the dust of the earth and as the stars of the sky in number. For this to be remotely possible Abraham and Sarah would need to give birth to a son and heir, and as they were both advanced in years this was well nigh impossible. In spite of the biological factor, God repeated His promise to Abraham that he would be the father of many nations. We now progress the story into Genesis 18 where in the midst of a remarkable conversation between the Lord God and Abraham concerning the birth of a son, we have recorded a prayer offered by Abraham that stands as a striking example of persistent prayer.

The Lord Speaks to Abraham
Genesis 18

Abraham had pitched his tent at Mamre. He was sitting at the door of his tent in the heat of the day when suddenly he is aware of the approach of three men. These three men stood before him, but these were no ordinary men, two of them were angels, and the other was the Lord Himself. We have recorded here a dramatic conversation, the details of which would have a profound impact upon the lives of Abraham and Sarah. The Lord was confirming to them that in spite of their advanced years, at the appointed time they would give birth to a son, the son of promise. This seemed at face value to be a statement of great incredulity, it caused Sarah to laugh at the prospect seeing that she was well beyond the years of childbirth. God responded to the doubt in Sarah's heart by reminding her and Abraham that nothing was impossible for Him to accomplish.

Suddenly, the whole tenor of the story changes. The Lord and the two angels look toward the wicked cities of Sodom and Gomorrah, cities that had become notorious for the most debauched and abominable extremes of sinful behaviour. God looked down upon these cities and saw the wickedness that was so flagrantly manifested. Such was His indignation and fury at what He saw, He determined that judgment would be brought to bear upon these detestable cities. It is important to note in passing that as in the case of Sodom and Gomorrah, God sees everything that is going on. There is nothing that can be hidden from His all seeing eye,

> *Because the outcry against Sodom and Gomorrah is great, and because their sin is very grave, I am going to see the situation for myself.*
>
> Genesis 18:20 (N.K.J.V.)

The two angels turn away, but Abraham still stood before the Lord. Before we look at the persistence of Abraham's prayer, it is worth noting that this episode clearly illustrates how God hates every sin and that by nature He is a God who must judge sin in all its forms.

Prayer and Persistence

And Abraham came near and said, would you also destroy the righteous with the wicked?

Genesis 18: 23

Why was Abraham so concerned?

Abraham's nephew Lot and his family were living in Sodom. Back in Genesis 13 we read that strife came between the herdsmen of Lot and the herdsmen of Abraham resulting in a parting of the ways. Lot chose the well watered Plain of the Jordan Valley and eventually settled his family in Sodom. Although there had been this separation, Abraham was greatly concerned as to the personal safety of Lot and his family. In addition to this concern, Abraham was anxious that God be seen to balance His wrath with His other great attributes of justice and mercy. Abraham had no doubt as to the gross sin of these cities and that God's wrath was justified, nevertheless the heart of Abraham yearned for the protection of the righteous. It was this great concern that led Abraham to embark upon a prayer that is marked as a prayer of persistence.

The Thrust of the Prayer

Suppose there were fifty righteous within the city; would you also destroy the place and not spare for the fifty righteous that were in it?

Genesis 18:24 (N.K.J.V.)

Not only is Abraham praying with great passion and determination, he is also praying with great skill. He knows at the outset that there were not fifty righteous people in Sodom, it was a city that was totally given over to the most debased forms of sexual perversion.

Persistence and Boldness

> *Far be it from you to do such a thing as this, to slay the righteous with the wicked. So that the righteous should be as the wicked, far be it from you! Shall not the judge of all the earth do right?*
>
> Genesis 18:25 (N.K.J.V.)

There was a determination on the part of Abraham to press through to God. At no time was Abraham taking liberties, he maintained his understanding that God was supreme in all matters and that He would act in accordance with His sovereign will and purpose. This understanding of God's nature actually became the motivating force behind Abraham's prayer on behalf of the handful of righteous people in the city.

"Shall not the judge of all the earth do right?" This question posed by Abraham indicated that in the midst of his passionate and persistent prayer, he possessed a growing trust in God that He would act justly in the treatment of all people, and that He would not be indifferent to the position of the righteous. The nature and character of God would always ensure that mercy would be shown to those who obeyed Him!

What lesson can we learn from Abraham's Prayer?

Abraham was able to engage in prayer on this level because he cultivated a close relationship with God. God had spoken to him on many occasions concerning the promise of a son, and this vital relationship was undergirded by a "covenant" promising blessing upon Abraham and his offspring. It was upon the basis of this relationship that Abraham was convinced that God would always balance justice with mercy and grace.

Believers today can experience this same level of intimacy with God particularly in the light of all that Jesus Christ has accomplished for us through the cross. Jesus no longer regards us as servants but as friends, this therefore must have profound implications when engaging in prayer on behalf of the needs of nations, communities and individuals.

What was God's initial response to Abraham's Prayer?

> *If I find in Sodom fifty righteous within the city, then I will spare all the place for their sakes.*
>
> Genesis 18:26 (N.K.J.V.)

Abraham's Prayer
Humility

Abraham is crying to God from the heart, but he is also praying with a great degree of humility as he submits his petition to the sovereign will of God. Consider the following phrases that form such an integral part of his prayer,

"I who am but dust and ashes" – "Let not the Lord be angry, and I will speak" – "Indeed now, I have taken it upon myself to speak."

Genesis 18:27

As we engage in persistent prayer before God, it is essential that we do so in a spirit of humility, submitting ourselves to God's will and counsel revealed to us in scripture.

50 – 45 – 40 – 30 – 20 – 10

No, these are not Abraham's lottery numbers! Here we see evidence of the incredible passion and persistence with which this great man prayed. This prayer of Abraham's must be a source of powerful encouragement to those who would seek to engage with God at this level. Far from God looking upon this prayer as an impertinence on Abraham's part, He rejoiced as He saw His servant grow in boldness and confidence as this prayer took on number crunching proportions. This is an important lesson for us as we pray. We must never approach God in fear or think that we are failing to observe His great majesty and power, no, God delights as we in confidence and boldness approach Him as Father and in faith engage Him at this level. Those of us who are parents take great delight when our children approach us in this way, particularly in their infant and childhood years, the same is true of God as we pour our hearts out to Him in prayer.

God's Promise

A most wonderful response at the end of Abraham's prayer,

I will not destroy it for the sake of ten.

Genesis 18:32 (N.K.J.V.)

58

At this point Abraham had the assurance that God would spare the small band of righteous people in the city and that Lot and his family would be safe.

God's judgment came

God destroyed Sodom and Gomorrah on account of the gross wickedness that was a hallmark of their daily lives and conduct. but in an act of great mercy and love, He spared the lives of Lot and his family.

Persistence: Praying for the Lost

In view of the judgment about to engulf our world, we need to be persistent in our prayers for the ingathering of the harvest.

Prayer and Persistence
Jacob: Genesis 32

Another powerful example of persistence in prayer is found in this amazing incident in the life of Jacob as he literally wrestled with God in prayer.

Jacob the "Trickster"

The fact that Jacob is given such a prominent place among the "greats" of God is due in no small measure to the mercy that the Lord conferred upon him. Jacob in his early years was an unsavoury character who would stop at nothing in order to gain an unfair advantage over even members of his own family. The term "trickster" paints an accurate picture of this man, he would in present day language be bracketed with a "second hand car salesman" in the league table of those who one would least trust. Jacob was a devious man who could not be trusted in that deception was his prime trait.

Born to Isaac and Rebekah near Beersheba in Southern Canaan, Jacob even from infancy, displayed his deviant character. He was the younger of his twin brother Esau, but in a blatant act of greed he persuaded Esau to sell him his birthright for a mere portion of meal. Then, to make matters worse, Esau was deceived out of his father's blessing through the combined trickery of Jacob and his mother Rebekah. Isaac, near to death, requests that the firstborn Esau go out into the field and hunt some game for him so that he could eat his favourite meal and then bless Esau before his death. Rebekah loved Jacob more than Esau and wanted Jacob to receive the blessing that legitimately belonged to Esau. Through an act of gross dishonesty, Jacob, whilst his brother Esau was away hunting, takes two choice goats and prepares savoury food for his father Isaac. Jacob, taking advantage of his father's blindness, presents the choice food to Isaac, and Isaac is taken in by the deception of the younger son. In Esau's absence Isaac confers the blessing of the firstborn upon Jacob. Esau returns from his hunting expedition only to discover that Jacob had once again conned him out of the blessing that should have been his. Esau, in a state of great distress, vows to kill his brother Jacob. Rebekah sends Jacob away for his own protection to Padan-Aram where he would find employment with his uncle Laban.

Jacob continued to live a life of deception and trickery even whilst he was in the employ of Laban. It was during this period that God began to deal with Jacob marking the beginning of a process of transformation in his life. As he was journeying toward Haran, he stopped overnight at a deserted outpost. He took a stone and used it as a pillow and there fell into a deep sleep. In the night Jacob saw a vision in which he saw a ladder set up on the earth with its top reaching to heaven. The angels of God were ascending and descending on it. God was standing above the ladder speaking directly to Jacob,

> *I am the Lord God of Abraham your father and the God of Isaac, the land on which you lie I will give it to you and your descendants.*
>
> Genesis 28:13 (N.K.J.V.).

God promised to bless the descendants of Jacob and that in number they would be as the dust of the earth, and that in his seed all the families of the earth would be blessed. God promised him His presence wherever he would go and that God would bring him back into the land reserved for him. Jacob awoke and immediately realised that he had been in the presence of God and subsequently named the place; "Bethel, The House of God." This marked the beginning of the transformation in Jacob's experience as God began to remove from him the traits that had been so offensive in his formative years.

Jacob served Laban in Padan-Aram for fourteen years and there married his wives; Leah and Rachael.

Wrestling in Prayer

We pick up the story now in Genesis 32. Jacob desires to mend fences with his estranged brother, Esau, and takes steps designed to bring about reconciliation. In the process of preparing for this encounter with Esau, Jacob experiences an incident that would change his life forever. He is anxious concerning his proposed meeting with Esau, he knows that Esau is coming to meet him with four hundred men, and it would seem that Esau was about to exact revenge upon Jacob. Jacob cries to God for protection and that He would deliver him from the hand of his brother. Jacob takes his wives, his children, and his servants and crosses the ford of Jabbok,

> *Then Jacob was left alone; and a man wrestled with him until the breaking of day.*
>
> Genesis 32:24 (N.K.J.V.).

Here we have a situation in which Jacob finds himself literally in a struggle with God. Such was the intensity of this struggle the socket of Jacob's hip was put out of joint. These moments were to be for Jacob the moments in which his life was to be totally transformed and his old devious nature put behind him,

> *And he said, let me go, for the day breaks. But he said, I will not let you go unless you bless me!*
>
> Genesis 32:26 (N.K.J.V.).

This determination on the part of Jacob was part of the process that God was masterminding in preparing Jacob for future service. The time had now come for Jacob to step into the purposes of God and to begin to realise his potential.

Transformation through Persistence

> *And he said, you shall no longer be called Jacob, but Israel; for you have struggled with God and with men, and have prevailed.*
>
> Genesis 32:28 (N.K.J.V.).

This incident marked a new beginning for Jacob. The name change heralded the final departure from the identity of the old Jacob. The person who was known for his cunning deviousness was now centre stage in the plans and purposes of God. The experience of Jacob provides us with a graphic illustration of God's redeeming and saving grace.

"Israel" – "Prince with God"

This change came about following Jacob's persistent wrestling with God. It is important to note that Jacob had firstly to be broken before God could bless him. The dislodging of the socket of Jacob's hip was part of the breaking process that had to happen so that he could move on to the next stage of his walk with God.

The Prayer of Persistence

Prayer on this scale may well involve a wrestling in the presence of God. The great challenges facing the church of Jesus Christ today are not going to be met by little five minute prayers offered to God at our convenience. Persistent prayer must be on the agenda of individual believers, but also be part of the life and pulse of the local church.

Persistent prayer is the dimension of prayer that must be entered into if we are going to see the great harvest gathered in. The prime motive of our praying must at all times be the salvation of the lost.

The Dynamics of Effective Prayer

Chapter 4

Prayer and Penitence

One of the foundational truths of the Christian gospel is that of the unconditional forgiveness of the sinner. The sacrificial work of Jesus Christ upon the cross has provided a means through which God can grant mercy and grace to the seeker. If there were to be any doubt concerning this great truth, then the whole fabric of salvation would lie in ruins. It must be said that forgiveness is not granted through prayer alone, there must be a clear understanding on the part of the penitent that pardon can only be given through the shed blood of Jesus. This is a theme that must be clearly taught in our churches today. There has been reluctance in recent years, on the part of many leaders, to preach about the blood of Jesus. Many leaders have abdicated their responsibility in this regard for fear of "offending" those who consider any mention of blood to be barbaric. Herein lies one of the principal reasons behind the decline in the power and authority of the church in the West. It is essential that this trend is reversed and that once again this great theme is clearly taught,

In whom we have redemption through his blood, the forgiveness of sins, according to the riches of his grace.

Ephesians 1:7 (N.K.J.V.)

The prayer of the penitent is a prayer that will always be lovingly received by Father God. His grace and mercy will immediately swing into action thus bringing unconditional forgiveness to the seeker. Not only is this form of prayer such a vital link in the process of coming to faith in Christ, but it is a powerful resource in the daily walk of the believer. Salvation does not make the Christian perfect, there is the constant struggle with the impulses of the flesh. Paul talks in terms of the flesh at war with the Spirit and the Spirit with the flesh, and there will be times in which the flesh will gain the upper hand. Thank God there is a means by which this can be overcome,

If we confess our sins, he is faithful and just to forgive us our sins and to cleanse us from all unrighteousness.

1 John 1:9 (N.K.J.V.)

Just prior to this verse, John reminds us that if we walk in the light as He is in the light, we have fellowship one with another, and the blood of Jesus Christ His Son cleanses us from all sin! This whole dimension of forgiveness from sin through the atoning work of Jesus Christ on the cross must be clearly understood if salvation is going to take root in the human heart.

We are going to examine in this chapter some notable examples in which forgiveness was granted in response to the prayer of the penitent.

The Prayer of the Penitent David: Psalm 51

In this Psalm we have one of the most powerful expressions of penitence ever uttered by an individual. David's plea for mercy comes from a heart that has been broken not only on account of personal sin, but a realisation that his transgression has been committed against God.

David's Adultery with Bathsheba 2 Samuel 11

This incident in the life of David contains some important lessons for every believer who engages in daily battle against Satan and his forces. Here we have a situation in which David; "The Lord's Anointed," the one chosen to be king, is suddenly overcome by a spirit of lust. When this incident occurred, David was at the height of his powers. Not only had God delivered him from the hand of Saul, but He had also given him great military victories over his enemies.

In addition to this, God had entered into a covenant with David promising him that his kingdom would be established forever. It would seem that David was in an unassailable position, with a guarantee of God's protection and blessing.

It was springtime, traditionally the time of year when kings engage in battle. David had always led his army into battle, but on this occasion he delegated the task to Joab, one of his commanders. There is a telling phrase in this narrative, a phrase that would have serious consequences for David,

But David remained at Jerusalem.

2 Samuel 11:1

67

Instead of leading his army into battle, David chose to enjoy the comforts of his surroundings. One evening, as David arose from his bed, he walked upon the roof of his house; something that under normal circumstances would seem to be a totally innocent pursuit. As he walked on his roof, his attention was drawn to another dwelling nearby. As he looked he saw Bathsheba, the wife of Uriah the Hittite, one of David's most loyal soldiers, taking a bath. Instead of looking away, David allowed himself to be overcome by a spirit of lust. He was about to embark upon a course of action that would have disastrous consequences for him and his family. David initiated an adulterous relationship with Bathsheba during which time her husband Uriah was fighting for him on the battlefield. As a consequence of this relationship, Bathsheba found herself to be pregnant thus setting in motion a series of events that would almost destroy David.

By this time, David's sense of judgment had all but deserted him, and in a fit of panic he engineers a set of circumstances designed to cover up his misdemeanor. Uriah, Bathsheba's husband, returned from the battle. David sought to persuade Uriah to go home and enjoy some "quality" time with his wife. David's hope was that during this brief interlude, Uriah and Bathsheba would have a sexual liaison so making it look as though the child Bathsheba was expecting was Uriah's. Not only is David now guilty of the sin of adultery, he compounds that with deception.

There are clear lessons to be learned from the conduct of David. He allowed himself to be in a situation of exposure to temptation when he should have been leading his army in battle. He opened the door for that lustful spirit to take root and to eventually dominate his actions. The Bible gives clear warning to guard against the strategies of the enemy in this whole area of sexual relationships. We are exhorted to guard the heart,

If I regard iniquity in my heart, the Lord will not hear.

Psalm 66:18

Guard the heart with all diligence, for out of it spring the issues of life.

Proverbs 4:23

For all that is in the world, the lust of the flesh, the lust of the eyes, and the pride of life, is not of the father, but of the world.

1 John 2:16 (N.K.J.V.)

David now finds himself in a downward spiral. In a desperate attempt to cover up his sin, David arranges for Bathsheba's husband, Uriah, to be placed at the forefront of the battle where the action would be at its most intense. He then gave instructions for protection to be removed from Uriah at the precise moment he came under enemy attack. Lust, adultery, deception, is now about to be added to by the sin of manslaughter as Uriah is quickly overcome in the heat of the battle. Following the news of her husband's death, Bathsheba is brought to the house of David, and she becomes his wife. David failed to remember that his duplicity, although hidden from his associates, could not be hidden from God's all seeing eye,

But the thing that David had done was evil in the eyes of the Lord!

2 Samuel 11:27 (N.K.J.V.)

This is a salutary lesson for us all, nothing can be hidden from the all seeing eye of God!

David's Sin Exposed
2 Samuel 12

God revealed to Nathan the Prophet the enormity of David's sin. The Prophet came to David and narrated a story concerning a rich man who had stolen from a poor man his only lamb in order to prepare a meal for himself. David, upon hearing this, expressed outrage at this conduct and ordered the offender to be put to death. Nathan then spoke words that cut to the heart of David,

Then Nathan said to David, you are the man!

2 Samuel 12:7

Nathan reminded David that God had anointed him to be king over Israel, and that He had delivered him from the hand of Saul, how could David do such evil in the sight of God?

David's conduct with Bathsheba and the ensuing events would have consequences for David and his family for years to come. God warned him that he would encounter adversity from within his own house, and that his wives would be sexually violated in public at the hand of his neighbour. David by his actions had dishonoured God and given the enemies of Israel a platform on which to blaspheme the Lord God. In one more solemn act of judgment, the child became ill and subsequently died.

Psalm 51

Here we have one of the great "penitential" Psalms of scripture. David penned it in response to his adultery with Bathsheba, and it constitutes a full and sincere expression of remorse for his sin. David, in writing this Psalm, acknowledges that he has suffered great loss as a result of his conduct, and he proceeds to set out the nature of these losses, presenting them before God in detail. This Psalm should be mandatory reading for the backslider seeking to find their way back to God. In the same way that God heard the cry from David's heart, so He will hear our heart cry also.

David's Losses
A Pure Heart

> *Have mercy on me, O God, according to your loving-kindness; according to the multitude of your tender mercies, blot out my transgressions. Wash me thoroughly from my iniquity and cleanse me from my sin.*
>
> Psalm 51:1-2(N.K.J.V.)

David was brought to a realisation that his foolish actions had deprived him of so much in terms of God's blessing and provision. He pleads for mercy, and he does so on the basis of God's loving-kindness. The prayer of the penitent will be devoid of excuses for sin, it will be a prayer of total contrition, and will be a cry for the mercy of God to be shown. David was painfully aware of his sin, the memory of it could not be erased, it was ever before him, and so from the heart he cries out; *"Blot out my transgressions; Lord, remove them for ever!"*

True Repentance
Psalm 51:3-7

David is coming to terms with the enormity of his sin. He acknowledges that it was entered into in the sight of God, and therefore it was against God that he had sinned and done this evil!

David's principal desire was for the restoration of a right heart relationship with God. In one of the great statements of scripture to do with the requirements that God looks for from those who claim to love Him, David states, *"Behold, you desire truth in the inward parts."*

The essence of what David is saying is that our relationship with God cannot be based solely upon our outward manner or disposition; God also clearly examines our character and conduct. The penitent, in coming before God in prayer, must recognise this important truth. David's passionate cry was for God to create within him a clean heart and that his spirit may be renewed.

David's Losses – Fellowship with God

> *Do not cast me away from your presence and do not take your holy spirit from me.*
>
> Psalm 51:11(N.K.J.V.)

David had enjoyed intimate fellowship with God particularly during times in which he found himself in personal danger. In the first chapter of this book we saw how Moses craved the presence of God, he could not envisage leading God's people into the Promised Land without the sure knowledge that God was with him. David experienced similar sentiments, whatever God might take away from him in the form of judgment, let it not be His Divine presence.

David's Losses – Joy

> *Restore to me the joy of your salvation, and uphold me by your generous spirit.*
>
> Psalm 51:12 (N.K.J.V.)

When a believer falls into sin and the fellowship link with God is broken, one of the first casualties caused by that breakdown is joy. Even the fleeting pleasure of sin cannot compensate for the joy the believer experiences as they walk before God in faith and obedience. David, on account of his sin had lost his joy, and he cries from the depth of his heart for that joy to be restored.

David's Losses – The Power to Witness

> *Then I will teach transgressors Your ways, and sinners shall be converted to You.*
>
> Psalm 51:13 (N.K.J.V.)

David had been an anointed leader in his daily life and witness, he possessed a powerful ability to engage with people concerning the mighty works of the God whom he served. This particular loss incurred by David, namely the power to witness, is so often experienced by believers today who succumb to the constant attack of the enemy. It may well be that effectiveness is eroded by the presence of habitual sin that just serves to sap the energy and passion for service. David's experience and the way in which he approached the situation, should be a source of great encouragement to us today. David, as he cried to God, found Him to be the God who not only forgives, but also restores. He is the God of the second chance, and He is the One who can restore the years the locusts have eaten.

David's Losses – Worship

David was known as the "Sweet Psalmist of Israel," he loved to spend time in the House of God singing His praises and basking in His presence. One of the prime casualties of unconfessed sin is our desire to worship. David, in one of his Psalms, reminds us that true worship can only be entered into by those who have clean hands and a pure heart, and those who have not lifted up their soul to an idol. David, therefore, realised that his capacity to worship had been severely diminished by his wanton sin,

> *Deliver me from the guilt of bloodshed, O God...and my tongue shall sing aloud of your righteousness. O Lord, open my lips, and my mouth shall show forth your praise.*
>
> Psalm 51:14-16 (N.K.J.V.)

David then goes on to define the true grounds for the restoration of the penitent,

> *The sacrifices of God are a broken spirit, a broken and a contrite heart – these, O God, you will not despise.*
>
> Psalm 51:17

God Hears the Prayer of the Penitent

God heard the cry of David and He hears our cry also. David had to be broken before God could take him to the next stage in his life. The penitent, in coming before God in true repentance, must experience that process of being broken before God, it is then, and only then that true restoration can fully take place.

There are several other notable examples of penitential prayer found in the pages of scripture all of which serve to clearly illustrate God's response in pouring His grace and mercy where breakdown had occurred.

Ezra – A Prayer of National Repentance

It is important to understand something of the background of Ezra's period of life and ministry. God had brought judgement upon the nation of Judah on account of her sin and rebellion. God had sent a succession of Prophets warning of impending wrath unless there was clear repentance. Failure to heed these warnings resulted in the nation being led away to captivity in Babylon. Jerusalem and the Temple were raised to the ground leaving the region desolate.

Seventy years were to pass before the Persian king Cyrus issued a decree for a remnant of the captives of Judah to return and rebuild the city of Jerusalem, and in particular the ancient Temple. The first company of returning exiles were led by Zerubbabel and were successful in laying the foundation of the new Temple. Opposition and gradual loss of vision took its toll and for sixteen years very little progress was made. After sixteen years the rebuilding was to re-commence under the influence of the Prophets Haggai and Zechariah.

Ezra leads a further company of returning exiles and assumes a position of spiritual leadership over them. Much of the work of restoration had been completed when a serious situation arose which required the attention of Ezra. He is approached by several of the leaders of the people who inform him that many of the returning exiles had intermarried with the heathen peoples of the land. This was a direct contravention to the law given by God to Moses concerning intermarriage.

Intermarriage Forbidden

Upon entry into the Promised Land, the Children of Israel were to destroy all pagan idols and worship sites, nor were they to enter into a form of covenant with the peoples of the land,

> *Nor shall you make marriages with them. You shall not give your daughter to their son, nor take their daughter for your son.*
>
> Deuteronomy 7:3 (N.K.J.V.)

It was brought to the attention of Ezra that this clear command had been flouted thus risking the judgement of God upon the returning exiles. Ezra, immediately recognising the gravity of the situation, calls the people together in order to express penitence and sorrow. Ezra, in an act of humility before God, tore his robe, plucked at some of the hair of his head and beard, and sat down astonished!

Ezra, on behalf of the people, takes the role of the penitent in humbling himself before God,

> *O my God, I am too ashamed and humiliated to lift up my face to you, my God; for our iniquities have risen higher than our heads, and our guilt has grown up to the heavens.*
>
> Ezra 9:6 (N.K.J.V.)

Ezra goes on to acknowledge that God had brought them back from Babylon, the land of captivity, and that He had granted them mercy and grace in the sight of the kings of Persia, and that He had enabled them to rebuild the House of God. Yet in spite of

God's faithfulness, the people had transgressed by entering into mixed marriages in direct contravention of His word.

Ezra's Penitent Prayer

As Ezra was praying, we read that he was weeping and broken before the Lord. He humbly acknowledges the sin of the people, and proceeds to make a covenant with God for the putting away of these pagan wives by whose influence the nation was in danger of slipping into idolatry.

Personal Responsibility

> *Arise, for this matter is your responsibility. We also are with you. be of good courage and do it.*
> Ezra 10:4 (N.K.J.V.)

This illustrates an important principle when engaging in the prayer of penitence. The sin of the individual is the responsibility of the individual and must be confessed by the individual. The people of Ezra's day had to take common ownership for their sin, and it was for each one to come before God in repentance.

Ezra proclaimed an edict throughout all Judah and Jerusalem for the people to gather together. The people stood before God in the pouring rain trembling in fear on account of their guilt. This is the mark of the true penitent.

Penitent Prayer Offered

Ezra reminds the people that they have transgressed in taking pagan wives,

> *Now therefore, make confession to the Lord God*
> *of your fathers, and do his will; separate*
> *yourselves from the peoples of the land, and*
> *from the pagan wives. Then all the assembly*
> *answered and said with a loud voice, yes! as we*
> *have said, so we must do.*
>
> Ezra 10:11-12 (N.K.J.V.)

The prayer of the penitent will always be followed up by action. They made their confession and then with a loud voice made a powerful expression of intent.

Nehemiah – Penitence on behalf of God's People

Nehemiah was the cup bearer in the Persian court of King Artaxerxes, a position that demanded that he at all times maintained a positive disposition. News is brought to him by men who had returned from Judah concerning the broken down state of the walls of Jerusalem. This information caused Nehemiah to break down in deep distress,

> *So it was, when I heard these words, that I sat*
> *down and wept, and mourned for many days; I*
> *was fasting and praying before the God of*
> *heaven.*
>
> Nehemiah 1:4 (N.K.J.V.)

Nehemiah, in his prayer, identified himself with the neglect of the people in their failure to rebuild the wall. There follows a powerful prayer of penitence in which Nehemiah cries to God on behalf of the people in confessing their sin and apathy.

Vicarious Prayer

> *Please let your ear be attentive and your eyes open, that you may hear the prayer of your servant which I pray before you now, day and night, for the children of Israel your servants, and confess the sins of the children of Israel...*
>
> Nehemiah 1:6 (N.K.J.V.)

Nehemiah also acknowledges the warnings given by God to Moses concerning the consequences of national sin; there would be a scattering amongst the nations. There was also that clause which expressed God's intent to restore His people in response to their confession of sin and of their humble and contrite return to His ways. Nehemiah's penitential prayer is based upon the fact that he was praying on behalf of the people of God, and that God would be attentive to this prayer and grant him favour in the presence of the king.

This prayer of Nehemiah became the catalyst by which the walls of the city were rebuilt in the face of great opposition.

Jonah

The Prophet Jonah was called by God to preach to the wicked city of Nineveh, a city known for its barbaric cruelty. The story is familiar to us; Jonah, overcome by fear, flees from the presence of God and boards a ship bound for Tarshish. A great storm batters the boat and Jonah is thrown overboard and is swallowed by a great fish. The fish spews Jonah onto the shore, and Jonah realises that he must be obedient to the call of God and preach in Ninevah. His message was simple,

> *Yet forty days, and Ninevah shall be overthrown.*
>
> Jonah 3:4 (N.K.J.V.)

The people of Ninevah repent before God, proclaim a fast, and cry to Him for mercy. This penitential cry is taken up by the king as he also covers himself in sackcloth and ashes.

Prayer and Penitence

> Let man and beast be covered with sackcloth, and cry mightily to God; yes, let everyone turn from his evil way and from the violence that is in his hands. Who can tell if God will turn and relent, and turn away from His fierce anger, so that we may not perish.
>
> Jonah 3:8-9 (N.K.J.V.)

When God heard the cry of their hearts, He acknowledged their confession, and relented from the disaster that He said He would bring upon them.

Prayer and Penitence – The New Testament

Jesus had much to say concerning forgiveness and confession of sin.

The Prodigal Son
Luke 15

A young man who had kicked the traces, turning his back upon his father and family and going into the city to spend his inheritance. Whilst he had the money he was popular and people desired to be in his presence. His was the party scene and the bright lights. Eventually his good fortunes ran out and he fell upon hard times. His situation became so dire that he found himself working as a farm hand feeding the pigs. He was so desperate he would even resort to eating the food meant for the pigs!

Eventually he came to his senses, he realised that even the servants who worked in his father's house were better off than he. His response can be regarded as a prayer of penitence,

> *Father, I have sinned against heaven and before*
> *you, and I am no longer worthy to be called your*
> *son. make me like one of your hired servants.*
>
> Luke 15:18-19 (N.K.J.V.)

This cry from the heart became the impetus that brought joyful reconciliation between the young man and his father. Just as the father never gave up on the son, so our Heavenly Father is always willing to extend His mercy and grace.

The Pharisee and the Tax Collector – Luke 18

Jesus was seeking to expose the hypocrisy of the religious rulers particularly in their attitude to prayer. He contrasts the proud pretentious prayer of the Pharisee as he boasts his religious piety, with the humble heart cry of the tax collector.

The Pharisee's Pride

> *God, I thank you that I am not like other men;*
> *extortioners, unjust, adulterers, or even as this*
> *tax collector. I fast twice a week; I give tithes of*
> *all that I possess.*
>
> Luke 18:11-12: (N.K.J.V.)

The tax collector, standing afar off, overcome by his sense of guilt, would not so much as even raise his eyes to heaven, but smote upon his breast, saying,

> *God be merciful to me a sinner!*
> Luke 18:13

The Verdict of Jesus

The tax collector went down to his house justified rather than the proud Pharisee! He who exalts himself shall be abased, and he who humbles himself shall be exalted.

The Prayer of the Penitent Thief – Luke 23

This perhaps is the most powerful example of penitential prayer found in the whole of scripture. The scene is the crucifixion of Jesus. He is in agony as He endures the taunts of the onlookers,

> *"If you are the Christ, save yourself and us!"*

This was not only the cry of the passers by, but it was the taunt of one of the two thieves crucified on either side of Him. The other criminal in his dying moments recognised the significance of the moment. The man on the centre cross was no ordinary man, He was certainly no criminal, and had done nothing deserving of death. The dying thief rebuked his fellow criminal,

> *Do you not even fear God, seeing you are under*
> *the same condemnation?*
> Luke 23: 40

As far as this criminal was concerned Jesus had done nothing wrong and His death was a major miscarriage of justice.

The Cry of the Penitent

> *Then he said to Jesus, Lord, remember me when you come into your kingdom. And Jesus said to him, assuredly, I say to you, today, you will be with me in paradise.*
>
> Luke 23:42-43 (N.K.J.V.)

Here we have the immediate response of Jesus to the cry of the penitent thief.

Today we can have the assurance that God still hears the prayer of the penitent and will immediately respond.

The Dynamics of Effective Prayer

Chapter 5

Prayer and the Prophetic

A volume such as this can never adequately do justice to this vast subject of prayer. Down through the centuries of church history, eminent scholars have written extensively on this great theme, many of their works have been regarded as "classics" in the field of Christian literature. In recent years, the complete works of the great prayer author E.M. Bounds have been edited into one volume, a must read for anyone seeking to get to grips with this great subject.

When giving consideration to the chapter titles of this book, I felt constrained to include a chapter on prayer in the dimension of the Prophetic. As I began to research this topic, I soon began to realise that there are many instances recorded in scripture in which prayer is exercised in the context of Prophetic ministry. It would be impossible to include all of these in one chapter, so I have majored on four situations, all of which clearly illustrate the link which exists between these two great disciplines of ministry. Three of these involve events taken from the lives of kings, and one taken from the life and ministry of a Prophet.

We shall examine this in the following way;

Solomon / *Prayer*   The aftermath of Prophetic ministry.

Jehoshaphat / *Prayer* Paving the way for Prophetic ministry.

Hezekiah / *Prayer*   In partnership with Prophetic ministry.

Daniel / *Prayer*   The foundation for Prophetic ministry.

Prayer and the Prophetic – Solomon
The Aftermath of Prophetic Ministry
2 Chronicles 6

Although Solomon was not a Prophet, we have recorded in this passage of scripture a prayer containing a powerful prophetic dimension. It was a prayer uttered in the aftermath of the prophetic ministry of Nathan spoken over the life of David. In order to understand the contents of this prayer, we need to briefly examine the events which transpired in the early years of David's reign as King of Israel. God had firmly established David upon the throne and had given him supremacy over his enemies. As a matter of priority he had sought to return the Ark of God back to its rightful place. This was achieved amidst great pomp and celebration as the Ark was returned to the City of David. Following its return, David found himself in a position of great power and prestige. The nation was secure in that God had given him rest from his enemies. There remained one abiding passion in the heart of David and that was to build a permanent "House" dedicated to the worship of God, and a place where the ark could be placed securely.

David's Desire

> *The king said to Nathan the Prophet, see now, I*
> *dwell in a house of cedar, but the Ark of God*
> *dwells inside tent curtains.*

2 Samuel 7:2 (N.K.J.V)

Nathan's initial response was to tell David to do all that was in his heart, for God was with him. Although David's motives were honourable, they were not in line with the sovereign will and purpose of God. God spoke to Nathan stating that He would not permit David to build the House, for he was a man of war, and had shed blood. It would be the responsibility of David's son to build the House. God had never dwelt in a house, from the days in which He had delivered Israel from the bondage of Egypt up until that day, the presence of God had been made manifest in a tent and in a Tabernacle. God instructs Nathan to remind David of the blessings that He had lavished upon him, in that He had taken him from the sheepfold, from following the sheep, to a position in which he was the ruler of Israel, but he was not to be personally responsible for the erection of this House of Worship. This Prophetic statement was not designed to bar David from any involvement in the building of the House. David would play a prominent role in the provision of materials with which to build the structure, but the task would fall to his son Solomon.

The Dedication of the Temple
2 Chronicles 5-6

Solomon is now firmly established upon the throne of Israel, and the nation is at peace. He was responding to the charge given him by his father David.

Consider now, for the Lord has chosen you to build a house for the sanctuary; be strong and do it.

1 Chronicles 28:10 (N.K.J.V.)

It is worthy of note here that David did not react in a negative way when informed that he would not build the House. There must have been a modicum of disappointment in that this was something he had set his heart upon. David responded to the Prophetic word given him by Nathan and was willing to abide by it.

God's Blessing upon Solomon

Now Solomon the son of David was strengthened in his Kingdom, and the Lord his God was with him and exalted him exceedingly.

2 Chronicles 1:1 (N.K.J.V)

The temple is built and the day of dedication beckons with much in the way of planning and preparation undertaken.

The Dedication Ceremony
2 Chronicles 5

This was truly a magnificent occasion in the history of the nation of Israel. The ceremony was to be marked by a dramatic manifestation of the power and glory of God. Prior to God's intervention we read that the musicians and singers were as one in singing to the Lord, and there was a great sense of expectation as the crowds gathered for this amazing event.

Suddenly the ceremony was transformed as the great Temple was filled with the glory of God's presence. Such was the intensity of His power, the Priests could not stand to minister; the glory of the Lord filled the House of the Lord. Amidst scenes of unparalleled glory and majesty, Solomon, under the anointing of the Holy Spirit, prays a prayer of dedication, the contents of which refer back to the prophetic statement given by Nathan to David concerning the building of the House.

Nathan's prophecy is clearly referred to in the early stages of Solomon's prayer, but it must be said that Solomon's prayer also contained prophetic content in relation to the future events that would overtake Israel as a nation.

Prayer and the Prophetic
Solomon's Prayer – 2 Chronicles 6

We have in the content of this prayer some of the most majestic words recorded in scripture. Solomon begins by affirming the truth of God's words spoken to his father David. Then he declared the purpose behind the building of this great Temple; it was to be a place in which the worship of the God of Israel would be offered. It was to be the permanent resting place for the Ark of the Covenant, and it would be a place in which the glory of God would be manifest.

Solomon then goes on to magnify the Lord by declaring that He was the Lord God of Israel, that there was no God in heaven or on earth like Him, and that He was a God who constantly kept His covenant and mercy with those who walked before Him. It is worthy of note that all the great Prophetic prayers recorded in scripture include strong references to the glory and majesty of God. This is something that needs to be clearly understood in the prayer ministry of the church today. So often our prayers can be so taken up with personal need that we forget the great glory of the God we are praying to.

Solomon in his prayer is also careful not to let the ornate splendour of the Temple surroundings detract from the supreme glory of God's presence,

> *But will God indeed dwell with men on the*
> *earth? Behold, heaven and the heaven of*
> *heavens cannot contain you. How much less this*
> *temple which I have built!*
>
> 2 Chronicles 6:18 (N.K.J.V)

There follows a section of prayer that contains strong Prophetic currents in that much of the content refers to circumstances and events that would be apparent in the life of the nation of Israel. Solomon's prayer has echoes of the words spoken by Moses to the children of Israel recorded in Deuteronomy 28. In that passage God promises blessings on account of their obedience, and curses should they lapse into idolatry and rebellion. This prayer of Solomon's follows a similar pattern.

Defeat at the Hands of their Enemies

> *Or if your people Israel are defeated before an*
> *enemy because they have sinned against you,*
> *and return and confess Your Name, and pray*
> *and make supplication before You in this*
> *Temple, then hear from Heaven, and forgive the*
> *sin of Your people Israel, and bring them back to*
> *the land which You gave to them and their*
> *fathers.*
>
> 2 Chronicles 6:24-25 (N.K.J.V)

This prayer was Prophetic in that it made provision for what the nation should do in the event of God's judgement being poured out on account of sin, resulting in defeat and certain captivity. This was to happen both at the hands of the Assyrians and the Babylonians. In the case of the Babylonian captivity which lasted for a period of seventy years, God would release His people and send them back to Judah and Jerusalem with the express purpose of rebuilding the Temple which had been totally destroyed by the Babylonian armies.

Pestilence, Blight and Mildew

Solomon's prayer also refers to the possibility of the heavens being shut up and there being no rainfall in the land. This came to pass in the days of Elijah as a direct result of God's judgment upon wicked King Ahab. These conditions are closely linked with the eventuality of pestilence, blight, and mildew,

> *When there is famine in the land, pestilence or blight or mildew, locusts or grasshoppers; when their enemies besiege them...whatever the plague or sickness...whatever prayer and supplication is made by anyone, or by all your people Israel...then hear from heaven Your dwelling place, and forgive their sin...*
>
> 2 Chronicles 6:28-30 (N.K.J.V)

In future years the nation would be blighted by the forces of nature and the infestation of locusts as God would bring His judgment to bear for their refusal to repent of sin.

The Fighting of Battles

Although Solomon was a man of peace and was not called upon to lead Israel in warfare during his reign, he had impressed upon his spirit that there would be seasons of conflict in which the nation would be called upon to engage their enemies on the battlefield. Solomon directs his prayer thus,

> *When Your people go out to battle against their enemies wherever You send them, and when they pray to You towards this city which You have chosen and the Temple which I have built for Your name, then hear from heaven their prayer and supplication, and maintain their cause.*
>
> 2 Chronicles 6:34-35 (N.K.J.V)

The prayer continues very much in the pattern of repentance, confession, and restoration. Although it must be stressed that Solomon was not a Prophet, his prayer contains much by way of Prophetic content. He was clearly being directed by the Holy Spirit as he prayed, and it was a prayer that flowed from the heart. Prophetic prayer will always be prayer expressed with great passion and intensity as it is a form of prayer undertaken usually on behalf of others.

How did God respond to this prayer?

> *When Solomon had finished praying, the fire came down from heaven and consumed the burnt offering and the sacrifices; and the glory of the Lord filled the Temple.*
>
> 2 Chronicles 7:1 (N.K.J.V)

As on the occasion of the dedication of the Temple, the priests once again were unable to minister because of the glory of the Lord that filled the House.

Prayer and the Prophetic – Jehoshaphat
Prayer that Paves the Way for Prophetic Ministry
2 Chronicles 20

Just over one hundred years have elapsed since Solomon prayed at the dedication of the Temple. Much has happened to Israel in the intervening years. The land has been split with the ten tribes forming the Northern Kingdom, and the tribes of Judah and Benjamin making up the Southern Kingdom. Jehoshaphat, King of Judah, finds himself in a situation in which the whole future of Judah is cast into doubt. Jehoshaphat faces a threat from the combined armies of Ammon, Moab, and Mount Seir.

In response to this threat, Jehoshaphat prays a prayer that paves the way for the dramatic intervention of Prophetic ministry.

Background Information

Jehoshaphat was the fourth king to reign upon the throne of Judah. Whilst there were some errors of judgement during his reign, his kingship was marked by a determination to be obedient to the God whom he served. He sought to walk in the ways of his "Father" David, and he was imbued with a determination to rid the land of all the areas of pagan worship. He took great delight in the ways of the Lord and as a result of his desire to follow the Lord, the land enjoyed a period of rest and calm.

Such was the level of blessing upon Jehoshaphat, the fear of the Lord fell upon all of the surrounding nations so that no nation would make war against Judah. Not only did he prosper in terms of military stature, he instituted a programme of reform in the nation which included a complete overhaul of the judicial system. He appointed Judges who would travel the land bringing their wisdom to bear upon all legal matters.

Threatened by Three Armies

The experience of King Jehoshaphat provides for us a mirror image of the warfare encountered by every believer. The Christian can experience times of blessing when it seems that everything in the 'Spiritual Garden' is rosy. Inevitably this gives way to seasons in which faith is tested and we are conscious of the attack of the enemy. This was the experience of Jehoshaphat. Just when it seemed that the nation was at peace, and that he himself was in a position of total security, enemy forces in the shape of three confederate armies appear on the horizon determined to inflict cruel defeat. It is interesting to observe the way in which Jehoshaphat reacts to this threat.

A Call to Prayer

> *And Jehoshaphat feared, and set himself to seek the Lord, and proclaimed a fast throughout all Judah. So Judah gathered together to ask help from the Lord; and from the cities of Judah they came to seek the Lord.*

> 2 Chronicles 20:3-4 (N.K.J.V)

Jehoshaphat soon realised that this threat could not be met by means of a military response, he was heavily outnumbered, and the armies of Judah would have been roundly defeated. On the contrary, Jehoshaphat embarked upon a strategy that we see increasingly all over the world today. He called multitudes of people from all parts of the nation to a central location to pray.

One of the most prominent features of the great prayer movement that God is building today is the coming together of great companies of people with the express purpose of calling upon God for the salvation of nations and communities. Nations that are today experiencing revival have seen prayer events such as these on a regular basis, and God has clearly responded to the heart cry of His people as He did in the days of the King of Judah.

The Nation at Prayer

> *So Judah gathered together to ask help from the Lord: and from all the cities of Judah they came to seek the Lord.*
>
> 2 Chronicles 20:4 (N.K.J.V)

There follows a prayer that comes straight from the heart of King Jehoshaphat, a prayer of passion and purpose, a mode of prayer that is urgently needed given the challenge facing the church today.

Prophetic Prayer
Acknowledging God for who He is

> *O Lord God of our fathers, are You not God in heaven, and do You not rule over the kingdoms*

> *of the nations, and in Your hand is there not power and might, so that no one is able to withstand You?*
>
> 2 Chronicles 20:6 (N.K.J.V)

The structure of this prayer contains some vital principles that we need to take on board when engaging in prayer on this level. So very often we make the mistake of coming before God simply to present to Him our requests. It seems that at times we almost treat Him like a vending machine; we make our request and we expect Him to respond immediately with the answer! Faith can only be engendered as we firstly focus on God for who He is. As we do this, our faith rises, and there is birthed within our spirit an expectancy that God has heard and will respond in accordance with His will and purpose. It is essential that our prayers are mingled with expressions of worship. Paul exhorts us to bring our requests with thanksgiving.

Jehoshaphat continues to pray with great skill and understanding. He reminds God of the promises made to His people should they ever be attacked by their enemies. He makes reference to the promise made to Abraham affirming that the land in which they dwell was promised to Abraham and his descendants as an ever-lasting possession.

Praying the Promise

> *If disaster comes upon us – sword, judgement, pestilence or famine – we will stand before His temple and in Your presence (for Your name is in this temple), and cry out to you in our affliction, and You will hear and save.*
>
> 2 Chronicles 20:9 (N.K.J.V)

Jehoshaphat's prayer of faith is prayed on two levels; not only did it refer to God's greatness and power, but it also was a prayer undergirded by the promises God had spoken to His people in previous generations.

Faith and Trust in God

Faith must always be accompanied by a total trust in God's absolute authority,

> *O our God, Will You not judge them? For we*
> *have no power against this great multitude that*
> *is coming against us; nor do we know what to*
> *do, but our eyes are upon You.*
>
> 2 Chronicles 20:12 (N.K.J.V)

The thrust of this prayer was that unless God intervened on behalf of His people, defeat would ensue, and His great name would be dishonoured. There are lessons for the church in this regard also. If we seek to fight the enemy by means of our programmes, our events, our conferences, and our endless diet of seminars, failure will inevitably ensue. This is not to say that these things do not have their place and can indeed be a means of blessing, but without the power and presence of the Living God in her midst, the church will continue to struggle.

The breakthrough was to come through the direct intervention of the Holy Spirit who came in response to the prayer of Jehoshaphat.

Prophetic Prayer and the Holy Spirit

At the end of Jehoshaphat's prayer, as all Judah with their wives and children stood before the Lord, the power of the Holy Spirit rested upon Jahaziel as he stood in the midst of the congregation.

Prophetic Prayer gives birth to the Prophetic Message

As this powerful anointing rested upon Jahaziel, the Lord revealed the strategy that was to be employed in defeating the enemy, it was a strategy that holds true for God's people today as we engage the enemy.

A Message of Hope

> *Listen, all you of Judah and you inhabitants of Jerusalem, and you, King Jehoshaphat! Thus says the Lord to you: Do not be afraid nor be dismayed because of this great multitude, for the battle is not yours but God's.*
>
> 2 Chronicles 20:15 (N.K.J.V)

Every believer at regular intervals in their walk with God will face the onslaught of the enemy, it is part and parcel of the experience of the disciple of Jesus Christ. One of the most effective ways to meet this challenge is by constantly reminding ourselves that the battle is not ours, it is the Lord's, and that He has promised to stand with us.

The Promise of Victory

> *You will not need to fight this battle, position*
> *yourselves, stand still and see the salvation of*
> *the Lord who is with you, O Judah and*
> *Jerusalem! Do not fear or be dismayed;*
> *tomorrow go out against them, for the Lord is*
> *with you.*
> 2 Chronicles 20:17 (N.K.J.V)

Jehoshaphat, in response to the Prophetic word, bowed his head
with his face to the ground, and all the people of Judah and
Jerusalem bowed before the Lord in an act of worship. A great
anthem of praise ascended to the Lord led by the Levites. A spirit
of faith was beginning to grip the hearts of the people and this
inspired Jehoshaphat to declare with great boldness,

> *Hear me, O Judah and you inhabitants of*
> *Jerusalem, believe in the Lord your God, and*
> *you shall be established, believe in His Prophets*
> *and you shall prosper.*
> 2 Chronicles 20:20 (N.K.J.V)

Following this powerful statement, Jehoshaphat appointed an
army of singers who would sing to the Lord and who would walk
in advance of the army of Judah. Their song was very simple, but
it was a declaration of the power and authority that belonged to
God and Him alone,

> *Praise the Lord, for His mercy endures forever.*
> 2 Chronicles 20:21 (N.K.J.V)

The Victory Accomplished

When the people began to praise the Lord, He set ambushes against each of the three confederate armies. Such was the confusion within the ranks of these armies, they turned upon each other and ended up killing each other. Jehoshaphat and his army did not need to lift a finger in anger against the enemy. God, in response to the prayer of Jehoshaphat, and the Prophetic directive given by Jahaziel, wrought victory for Judah that day.

Jehoshaphat's Prayer

A prayer that paved the way for Prophetic ministry!

Prayer and the Prophetic – Hezekiah
Prayer in partnership with Prophetic Ministry
2 Kings 19

The events surrounding the reign of King Hezekiah of Judah provide for us another powerful example of this great link that exists between prayer and the Prophetic. Hezekiah found himself in a similar situation to Jehoshaphat in that he was threatened by a vastly superior army under the leadership of Sennacherib, King of Assyria. Prayer, as in the case of Jehoshaphat, became the key to securing victory.

Background Information

Hezekiah came to power during a period in which Judah as a nation had turned away from God and had become engrossed in idolatry. Through the sin of his father, Ahaz, pagan worship had taken hold in the nation and the Temple of God had been

100

profaned. It was into this situation of great darkness that Hezekiah ascended the throne at the age of twenty five. His priorities were very clear, he sought to do what was right in the sight of the Lord and took steps to rid the land of all sites of pagan worship. In addition to this he destroyed the wooden images dedicated to the worship of the god, Asherah. He also broke in pieces the bronze serpent that Moses had made because it had become an object of veneration to the people.

A Commendation

He trusted in the Lord God of Israel, so that after him there was none like him among all the kings of Judah, nor who were before Him.

2 Kings 18:5 (N.K.J.V)

Among his other major reforms was the re-instatement of the Feast of the Passover. Yet in spite of these major reforms, Hezekiah was to suddenly experience a season of great testing and trial. This came in the form of threats made by Sennacherib, King of Assyria. This ruthless leader had already led captive the ten tribes of the Northern Kingdom of Israel, and had penetrated Judah right up to the outskirts of the capital. As in the case of Jehoshaphat, Prophetic prayer was to be the key by which Hezekiah would be victorious.

The Inevitability of Attack

After these deeds of faithfulness, Sennacherib the King of Assyria came and entered Judah...

2 Chronicles 32:1 (N.K.J.V)

The experience of Hezekiah runs parallel to the experience of every Christian believer. So very often deeds of faithfulness and service for God are rewarded by periods of testing and trial when our faith is shaken to its roots. This is something that every child of God has to be ready for in that it is not "if" trials come, but "when" they come. James, in his New Testament epistle, gives us guidelines as to how we are to respond when such circumstances arise,

> *My Brethren, count it all joy when you fall into various trials, knowing that the testing of your faith produces patience.*
>
> James 1:2-3 (N.K.J.V)

These seasons of testing will always move us onto greater levels of maturity and wisdom.

Hezekiah's Initial Response
2 Kings 19

He was greatly alarmed at the prospect of being totally overrun by the superior armies of Assyria. In response to the threat, he tore his clothes, covered himself with sackcloth, and went into the house of the Lord.

A Bleak Outlook

> *...this is a day of trouble and rebuke, and blasphemy; for the children have come to birth, but there is no strength to bring them forth.*
>
> 2 Kings 19:3 (N.K.J.V)

Sennacherib then began to engage in psychological mind games with Hezekiah and the inhabitants of Jerusalem. His ploy was to cause them to doubt the ability of Hezekiah to provide effective leadership, and also to question God's protection in the face of the Assyrian army,

> *Do not let your God in whom you trust deceive*
> *you, saying, Jerusalem shall not be given into*
> *the hand of the King of Assyria.*
>
> 2 Kings 19:10 (N.K.J.V)

One of the most potent weapons employed by Satan in his warfare against the believer is to promote doubt concerning the whole question of God's ability or even desire to protect his people. This serves to erode faith and can very quickly lead to disaster.

Sennacherib's Boast

> *Have the Gods of the nations come to the rescue*
> *of those whom my father destroyed?*
>
> 2 Kings 19:12 (N.K.J.V)

The Assyrians had swept all before them, all opposition had been totally destroyed, and no "God" as yet had come to their aid.

Hezekiah could not afford to remain inactive. Much of Judah had already been taken, Jerusalem the capital was surrounded, this called for urgent prayer given that there could be no military response to this powerful threat. Upon receiving the message, Hezekiah went up to the House of the Lord, and spread the letter containing the threat before the Lord. He proceeds to offer a prayer that was a cry from the heart asking God to intervene in this great crisis. He knew that his prayer stood between God's people and total destruction.

Once again we have prayer prefaced by a declaration of God's absolute might and power,

> *O Lord God of Israel, the one who dwells*
> *between the cherubim, You are God, You alone,*
> *of all the Kingdoms of the earth. You have made*
> *heaven and earth.*
>
> 2 Kings 19:15 (N.K.J.V)

Hezekiah brings Sennacherib's threat before the Lord, a threat that constitutes an offence to the living God. The prayer goes on to review the carnage inflicted upon the surrounding nations; entire territories had been crushed, the gods whom men worshipped had been destroyed, all of this accompanied by acts of ruthless barbarism!

> *Now therefore, O Lord our God, I pray, save us*
> *from his hand, that all the kingdoms of the earth*
> *may know that You are the Lord God, You alone.*
>
> 2 Kings 19:19 (N.K.J.V)

The prime focus of Hezekiah's prayer was not simply a cry for preservation, it was a plea for the honour and majesty of the God of Israel to be upheld, not only in Judah and Jerusalem, but in all the territories plundered by the armies of Assyria.

"THAT YOU ARE GOD AND YOU ALONE"

This is a prayer that urgently needs to be declared from the lips of His church particularly in the nations of the West!

Prayer Prayed in partnership with the Prophetic
Isaiah

Following the prayer of Hezekiah and in conjunction with it, God gives revelation to the prophet Isaiah concerning the eventual outcome of this matter.

God Hears

> *Then Isaiah...said to Hezekiah, thus says the Lord God of Israel: Because you have prayed to me against Sennacherib King of Assyria, I have heard.*
>
> 2 Kings 19:20 (N.K.J.V)

Spanning verses 22-34 of 2 Kings 19, we have the great Prophetic revelation spoken by Isaiah in response to the prayer of Hezekiah. It is a message of deliverance and victory for Hezekiah and the inhabitants of Jerusalem.

Victory Assured

> *Therefore thus says the Lord concerning the King of Assyria: he shall not come into this city, nor shoot an arrow there, nor come before it with shield, nor build a siege mound against it. By the way that he came, by the same shall he return; and he shall not come into the city, says the Lord.*
>
> 2 Kings 19:32-34 (N.K.J.V)

The Victory Gained

Following this great prophetic declaration of Isaiah, the Angel of the Lord went out and in the camp of the Assyrians killed one hundred and eighty five thousand of their soldiers. The inhabitants of Jerusalem rose early in the morning and found the dead bodies scattered around the perimeter of the city. Sennacherib returned home in abject defeat and was eventually murdered by two of his sons. This incident illustrates the great power generated as prayer provides the pathway for the ministry of the prophetic.

Prayer and the Prophetic – The Prayer of Daniel
The Foundation for Prophetic Revelation

In terms of Prophetic Prayer, Daniel stands out as one of the most articulate exponents of such prayer. There are at least three incidents recorded in the book of Daniel that illustrate the profound influence that his prayers bought to bear upon major events.

Background Information

Daniel was one of the articulate and bright young Jewish captives deported to Babylon when Judah was attacked by their armies under the leadership of Nebuchadnezzar. Upon arrival in Babylon, Daniel's great ability was immediately noticed. He was set apart for specialist training in the language and literature of the Chaldeans. Daniel was offered favourable living conditions which included daily portions of the king's food, along with choice wines from the royal vintage. In addition to this he would have three years of intensive training which, upon graduation, would ensure Daniel an important post in the court of Babylon. Daniel refused to be swept aside with this opulence, he refused to compromise his testimony, and took his stand for righteousness and purity. He dared to refuse the royal delicacies and insisted upon a strict diet of vegetables and water. This same stand was taken by Daniel's friends; Hananiah, Mishael and Azariah.

Eventually Daniel and his three friends had their names changed; Daniel became Belteshazzer, Hananiah became Shadrach, Mishael became Meshach and Azariah, Abed-nego.

Nebuchadnezzar's Dream

The first major challenge that Daniel faced working as he did in the royal court is recorded in this second chapter. In the second year of his reign, Nebucadnezzar had dreams that greatly troubled him resulting in lost sleep. He gave a command to the magicians and astrologers of Babylon requiring them to interpret the meaning of these dreams. The magicians and astrologers were amongst the elite of the Babylonian court, they were men who were steeped in Chaldean folklore and were able with great accuracy to predict future events. It needs to be said in passing that their ability to operate in this way was largely due to their involvement in occultic practises.

The Chaldeans ask Nebuchadnezzar to relate to them the details of his dreams but he refused, it was for them to find out, and then to inform the King. This task was well nigh impossible; no such request had ever been made to the wise men of the realm. The situation became increasingly fraught given Nebuchadnezzar's threat to execute his astrologers if they failed to give him what he required.

The Astrologers' Plight

> *The Chaldeans answered the King, and said,*
> *there is not a man on earth who can tell the*
> *King's matter; therefore no king, lord or ruler*
> *has ever asked such things of any magician,*
> *astrologer or Chaldean.*
>
> Daniel 2:10 (N.K.J.V)

Nebuchadnezzar was furious and immediately gave instructions for the wise men of Babylon to be put to death. Daniel and his friends were to be included in this massive cull of magicians and astrologers.

Daniel, upon hearing of this, approached Arioch the captain of the King's guard asking why this panic on the part of Nebuchadnezzar. In an act of incredible bravery, Daniel approaches the King asking him to give time so that the interpretation of his dreams could be given. Daniel's request is granted, and he immediately returns to his three colleagues, and they come before God in fervent prayer,

> *That they may seek mercies from the God of*
> *heaven concerning this secret, so that Daniel*
> *and his companions might not perish with the*
> *rest of the wise men of Babylon.*
>
> Daniel 2:18 (N.K.J.V)

No amount of discussion or debate would suffice, prayer was to be the key to unlocking this urgent matter.

The Dream Revealed

Following this season of prayer, the secret of Nebuchadnezzar's dream was revealed to Daniel in a night vision. In response to this, Daniel blessed the God of Heaven with a prayer that contains a strong prophetic content,

> *Blessed be the name of God forever and ever, for wisdom and might are His. And He changes the times and the seasons; He removes kings and raises up kings, He gives wisdom to the wise and knowledge to those who have understanding. He reveals deep and secret things; He knows what is in the darkness, and light dwells with Him. I thank You and praise You, O God of my Fathers; You have given me wisdom and might, and have now made known to me what we asked of You, for You have made known to us the King's demand.*
>
> Daniel 2:20-23 (N.K.J.V)

This is a moment of great triumph for Daniel and his friends. He is able with confidence to stand before the King and declare that the wise men and astrologers of the court of Babylon, with all of their learning, were powerless to assist the King in this matter. Daniel is careful to give all the glory to God.

The Source of Daniel's Power

> *But there is a God in heaven who reveals secrets, and He has made known to the King what will be in the latter days.*
>
> Daniel 2:28 (N.K.J.V)

Daniel Interprets the Dream

In a powerful statement of Prophetic revelation, Daniel is able to interpret the King's dream. The dream related to four great Gentile Kingdoms, the first of which was Babylon. Nebuchadnezzar saw in his dream a great image, each part of the image was made up of varying qualities of metal, each of which were symbolic of these great Gentile Empires. Beginning with Babylon, Nebuchadnezzar saw the coming to power of the great empires of Medo-Persia, Greece and Rome. He was receiving a panoramic view of world history from his day up to and including events that would be taking place following the second coming of our Lord Jesus Christ.

God's Name Honoured

> *The King answered Daniel, and said, truly your God is the God of Gods, the Lord of Kings, and a revealer of secrets, since you could reveal this secret.*
>
> Daniel 2:47 (N.K.J.V)

The King promoted Daniel and gave him many gifts and appointed him ruler over the whole province of Babylon, and chief administrator of the wise men of Babylon. Daniel's friends, Shadrach, Meshach and Abed-Nego were also honoured and given prominent posts in government.

Prayer and the Prophetic

In examining this aspect of prayer one could probably have written another chapter, but the four instances that we have looked at have given us adequate understanding of the principles that are to the fore when engaging in prayer on this level.

The Dynamics of Effective Prayer

Chapter 6

Prayer
Taught and Modelled by Jesus

To attempt to write a book on this vast subject of prayer without making any reference to its role in the life and ministry of Jesus must surely be a futile exercise. We have examined in some detail instances recorded in the Old Testament of how the presence and power of God was manifest in response to prevailing prayer. We now begin to see how that prayer was a discipline of paramount importance to Jesus as He conducted His earthly ministry. Our objective is to see how Jesus taught and modelled prayer both in His private devotions alone with His Father, but also the part prayer played in His public ministry.

A careful study of the life and ministry of Jesus will reveal how that lives were dramatically changed following an encounter with Him. The gospel writers vividly portray His style of ministry, methods of communication, how He interacted with different people, and the impact He made upon entire communities. There were those who gladly received His message, but there were others who were openly hostile to Him. One thing is sure and that is that where Jesus went, crowds flocked to hear Him. They marvelled at His clarity and His authority. His approach was so different to the tawdry ministry style of the religious leaders of the day, they said of Him, *"Never man spake like this man."* People looked on in wonder as He defied the laws of nature by walking on the water and by causing the raging waves to be still. They were held in rapt attention as He expounded the message of the Kingdom of God by the use of Parables. They gazed in wonder as they saw Him raise the dead back to life and as He broke the power of sickness and infirmity. Put simply, the gospel writers relay the account of Jesus Christ, the Son of God, a man empowered by the Holy Spirit, who went about doing good, and healing all who were oppressed by the devil.

When considering the great impact the life and ministry of Jesus made upon people, the part that prayer played in the exercising of this role can never be underestimated. Jesus was clearly a man of prayer, it was the secret behind His power, and He never attempted any ministry situation before firstly spending quality time alone in prayer with His Father. Having spent time in prayer prior to engaging in ministry, Jesus would often return to the place of prayer following times of ministry,

> *And great multitudes came together to hear, and to be healed by Him of their infirmities. And He withdrew Himself into the wilderness and prayed.*
>
> Luke 5:15-16 (N.K.J.V.)

This passage recorded by Luke details an intense period of ministry undertaken by Jesus in which He manifested mighty power in healing the sick. Jesus recognised the importance of

114

spending time alone with His Father so as to await further instruction. There may well have been the temptation to stay with the multitudes and to be part of the great outburst of joy that was being expressed in response to these powerful miracles. No, for Jesus prayer was the priority.

The gospel writers go on to record how that Jesus engaged in prayer in the hours prior to daybreak and at sunset. He spent an entire night in prayer before appointing His disciples. He prayed in the presence of children reminding people of their vital role in the Kingdom of God. He prayed for Peter on the occasion of his denial, that failure would be followed by restoration to service.

Much could be written relative to the prayer life of Jesus, but in this chapter we are going to focus on what has been termed as His "Model Prayer."

The Lord's Prayer
Matthew 6, Luke 11

Matthew's account of the Lord's Prayer is included in the narrative which contains the Sermon on the Mount. At the beginning of Matthew 6, Jesus is teaching as to the correct motivation that must be shown when exercising charitable deeds. He also gives clear instructions as to the correct procedure required when engaging in such activities as prayer and fasting. He is at pains to expose the hypocrisy of the religious rulers, who, when engaging in such deeds, did so with great public acts of pride and pomposity. They would always pray and fast when there were crowds present whether it be in the Synagogues or in the public arena, these proud leaders excelled in acts of false piety. Such conduct was an offence in the eyes of God and incurred the displeasure of Jesus. In response to this detestable practise, Jesus gives clear teaching as to the right way in which charitable deeds should be undertaken. He also issues instructions to His disciples as to how they should engage in the disciplines of prayer and fasting.

The anger of Jesus can be clearly seen in His use of the word "Hypocrite,"

> *And when you pray, you shall not be like the hypocrites, for they love to pray standing in the synagogues and on the street corners, that they may be seen by men. Assuredly, I say to you, they have their reward.*
>
> Matthew 6:5 (N.K.J.V.)

This misconduct on the part of these "hypocrites" may have done wonders for their religious egos, but in the sight of God they were uttering mere empty words. Not only that, but most of the people looking on were not taken in by this, they viewed this charade with open disdain. Much religious orthodoxy and ritual practised by many today is identical to that of these leaders in Jesus' day, and He would issue strong words of rebuke today as He did two thousand years ago. Such acts of false piety will do nothing to further the cause of the Kingdom of God and will only serve as barriers to those who are genuine in their search for truth. Having exposed this grave error, Jesus then goes on to teach the correct approach to prayer. In particular He is referring to private acts of devotion entered into between the individual believer and Father God,

> *But you, when you pray, go into your room, and when you have shut the door, pray to your Father who is in the secret place; and your*

> *Father who sees in secret will reward you*
> *openly.*
>> Matthew 6:6 (N.K.J.V.)

There is something very powerful in this instruction given by Jesus in respect to private prayer. Firstly, He is clearly stating that the way is open for the believer to approach God in prayer. We must never come before God in a spirit of familiarity, there is too much of that type of approach in the church today, we must at all times have regard to His majesty and glory. Nevertheless, we are invited to come before Him with boldness, not in our own strength, but by means of the finished work of Christ on the cross.

The private prayer closet is a place of infinite value to the believer. Sadly today, very few of God's people have cultivated the discipline of finding a space and utilising it as their place of communion with Him. This is a practise that urgently needs to be rehabilitated in the life of the church and indeed in the life of every individual Christian. It can be the place in which God can reveal to us His plans for our future and the future of our families. Another benefit to accrue from entering into the private place is that it is a prayer dialogue between God and us. It acts as a safeguard should we ever be tempted to lapse into a spirit of pride as we engage in acts of worship.

Will Reward You Openly

Careful observation of these instructions given by Jesus relative to prayer will produce great dividends for the believer. The great heart of God longs to bless His people and to provide for their every need. We must never regard God as some "Scrooge" figure who reluctantly, and only when in a good mood, will pour blessing into the lives of His people. This is not the God we serve, He is One who delights to provide for His people in response to their love for Him and their obedience to His Word. He is aware of our every need and has promised to respond when we call upon Him. The only condition He lays down is that we *"Seek first the Kingdom of God and His righteousness."*

Dangerous Pitfalls

> *And when you pray, do not use vain repetitions as the heathen do. For they think that they will be heard for their many words.*
>
> Matthew 6:7 (N.K.J.V.)

The "hypocrites" that Jesus referred to here would love to pray using ornate phrases designed to impress people with their speaking skills, in other words; "Religious Jargon." This mode of prayer causes great offence to God and can be a turn off to young believers who are seeking to take their first steps in cultivating an understanding of prayer.

After having issued these basic guidelines in respect of prayer, Jesus then goes onto "model" a prayer that can be prayed by the youngest child and the most mature adult; commonly regarded as, "The Lord's Prayer." In the account written by Luke, Jesus teaches the prayer following a time of personal communion between Him and the Father. The disciples, observing this pattern of prayer in the life of Jesus, request Him to teach them to pray. Jesus responds by compiling this great prayer,

> *In this manner, therefore pray: our Father in heaven, hallowed be Your Name.*
>
> Matthew 6:6 (N.K.J.V.)

Many commentators have referred to this as 'The Model Prayer'. This may or may not be the case, but in any event, Jesus lays down some very firm principles that need to be observed when approaching the whole discipline of prayer.

"Our Father in Heaven"

There must firstly be a clear recognition of whom we are praying to. We are praying to our "Heavenly Father." It is vital that this is adhered to at all times. So very often the mistake is made in that we come before God with an immediate shopping list of requests. In our quest to receive from God, we fail to acknowledge Him for who He is. He knows our situation before we come before Him, He is aware of our needs. It is therefore an act of great disrespect to simply approach Him on the basis of our desires. The effectiveness of our prayer will be greatly enhanced as we come into a more mature understanding of the whole concept of the Fatherhood of God. When the believer grasps this great truth; namely that our Father in Heaven desires to bless us, and is keenly aware of every facet of our lives, then His provision and blessing will begin to be in evidence.

It is interesting to note how that the Apostle Paul in his epistles often makes reference to this great theme of the Fatherhood of God and of the blessings that flow when the believer comes into a greater understanding of who God is,

> *Blessed be the God and Father of our Lord Jesus Christ, who has blessed us with every spiritual blessing in the heavenly places in Christ.*
> Ephesians 1:3 (N.K.J.V.)

These blessings are numerous and cannot be counted. The scripture reminds us that our names are engraved upon the palm of His hands, and even the very hairs of our head are numbered.

"Hallowed be Your Name"

In coming before God in prayer, Jesus is telling His disciples to at all times "honour" God's Name. This is so vitally important as we seek to engage in prayer in our daily lives. We are living in days in which His Name is routinely blasphemed in the media and in the common street language of our towns and cities. Believers must take a stand against this tendency and be seen to object when such behaviour is in evidence. This stand may prove costly and could impinge upon our circle of friends etc., but if we truly revere His Name He will honour us. In praying this, we are asking that our Father's Name be held in high honour at all times and by all people.

"Your Kingdom Come"

This is a request that resonates in the heart of God whenever it is prayed. It is a statement that goes to the core of the mandate given to the church of Jesus Christ: namely to preach the gospel of the Kingdom. It begins with the words of John the Baptist as he sought to prepare the way for the coming of Jesus,

> *Repent, for the Kingdom of God is at hand.*
>
> Matthew 3:2 (N.K.J.V.)

Jesus Himself then takes up this theme as He commences His ministry,

> *Repent, for the Kingdom of Heaven is at hand.*
>
> Matthew 4:17 (N.K.J.V.)

120

This statement has major implications for the church as she seeks to fulfil the Great Commission given to the disciples by our Lord just prior to His ascension. The preaching of this great theme of the Kingdom of God is the weaponry made available to believers to confront the Kingdom of Darkness, a kingdom ruled over and directed by Satan himself. It is the same message preached by Jesus during His earthly ministry, and it is the same message declared by the Apostles following the dramatic events on the Day of Pentecost. The church has been empowered by the Holy Spirit to reach out to those whose lives have been blighted by the powers of darkness, that they also may experience the transforming life of the Kingdom of God.

In praying "Your Kingdom Come," we are engaging in prayer on two levels. Firstly, the Kingdom of God is present in and through the life and witness of the church as she seeks to proclaim this great commission. It is also present in the hearts of all who have come under the Lordship of Jesus Christ. Secondly, we pray "Your Kingdom Come" as an expression of anticipation relative to the future reign of Jesus Christ at the end of the age. This will mark the establishing of the Kingdom of God in all its eternal power and glory. Jesus will reign in supreme authority with Satan and all his forces consigned to everlasting destruction.

"Your Will be Done"

This is a natural consequence of the prayer; "Your Kingdom Come." The Kingdom of God is manifest as His Sovereign will and purpose is outworked in the hearts and lives of men and in the affairs of nations. When we look at this from a Heavenward perspective, we see a continuous demonstration of God's absolute will. Our understanding of Heaven is that it is a place of supreme glory where God dwells in unapproachable light, a place totally devoid of darkness or of any evil presence. In praying "Your will be done," we are anticipating the day when God's absolute and unchallenged will is present on earth as it is in Heaven! This request again anticipates the future glory of the full manifestation of God's Kingdom.

"Give us this Day our Daily Bread"

Jesus in teaching His disciples to pray has been careful to place great emphasis on acknowledging Father God for who He is, and for the honouring His Name. There now follows a section in this great prayer that takes the form of petitions. Jesus is seeking to establish in the minds of the disciples the fact that God is not some remote figure who is somewhat detached from the realities of everyday life. These petitions listed by Jesus are given so that we can have the assurance that God is vitally concerned as to our temporal needs, i.e. the necessities of daily life.

There is nothing more basic than bread, it is the staff of life, and our Father in Heaven is acutely aware of our need for daily provision. This is a principle that needs to be clearly understood as we approach God in prayer. Faith can be powerfully reinforced when we come to a firm understanding that the Almighty creator of the universe takes a vital interest even in our most basic needs. Jesus reminds us that even a sparrow cannot fall to the ground without the knowledge of Father God, and we are of much greater value than the sparrow.

There is however one caveat that we need to inject here, and that is that God is the One who meets our needs and not our wants. Nowhere in scripture are we exhorted to pray for items of luxury that may only lead to indolence or indulgence. This is not to deny that God is a God of superabundance and that there are times in which we receive of His providential blessing, but the thrust of this petition is to do with the daily necessities of life.

"And Forgive us our Debts"

Jesus in including this petition in His prayer is touching upon one of the foundational truths of the gospel of the Kingdom. When there is the heart cry for forgiveness based upon the act of repentance and contrition, God always hears. When the sinner comes to faith in Christ, there is that acknowledging of the presence of sin. This is accompanied by confession and a determination to turn away from sin in all its form. When the prayer of confession is offered, pardon and grace is freely given and the debt of sin is cancelled,

> *Therefore, having been justified by faith, we have peace with God through our Lord Jesus Christ.*
>
> Romans 5:1 (N.K.J.V.)

Paul in his epistle to the Ephesians sets out the position of the unbeliever prior to their conversion. He writes in stark terms in describing them as being; 'Dead in Trespasses' and under the judgement of a righteous God. In addition to this the unconverted person is weighed down by the 'Debt' of sin and has no means with which to settle that debt. The cross of Jesus Christ has served to reverse this impasse. Through His obedience to the will of His Father, Jesus has paid the price through the shedding of His blood, providing a means by which the "Debt" of sin can be cancelled. It is therefore with great assurance that this petition can be made and forgiveness extended.

This is not only given for the benefit of the sinner, it is a prayer that believers must pray on a regular basis. Salvation does not render us free from the constraints of the flesh. As believers we are waging warfare with a potent enemy who is bent upon our destruction, and who seeks to rob us of our confidence in God. Paul puts this so graphically in his letter to the Galatians,

> *For the flesh lusts against the Spirit, and the Spirit against the flesh; and these are contrary to one another, so that you do not do the things that you wish.*
> Galatians 5:17 (N.K.J.V.)

This petition is to be prayed by the believer when there is the awareness of unconfessed sin coupled with a desire to be right with God. It is a prayer that can be said in response to the accusations of Satan directed against the Christian. Everyone who confesses Jesus Christ as their Lord and Saviour will experience this conflict on a regular basis. Whilst there may be the desire to honour God in our daily walk and to live in accordance with His commands, failure will from time to time occur. Jesus allows for this eventuality by inserting this petition in His prayer. This request is echoed by the writings of the Apostle John in regard to the question of sin,

> *If we say that we have no sin, we deceive ourselves and the truth is not in us. If we confess our sins, He is faithful and just to forgive us our sins and to cleanse us from all unrighteousness.*
> 1 John 1:8-9 (N.K.J.V.)

John here is writing to believers, and his exhortation is in line with the petition spoken by Jesus for inclusion in this prayer.

"As We Forgive our Debtors"

We receive forgiveness through the grace and mercy of a loving God. It has nothing to do with the observance of religious ritual or ceremony, it is God extending His pardon to us through the work of His Son Jesus on the cross. Having been the recipients of this free grace, we in turn should always be ready to forgive those who sin against us. This principle is clearly taught by Jesus in response to a question asked of Him by Peter,

> *Then Peter came to Him and said, Lord, how often shall my brother sin against me, and I forgive him? Up to seven times? Jesus said to him, I do not say to you, up to seven times, but up to seventy times seven.*
>
> Matthew 18:21-22 (N.K.J.V.)

Jesus goes on to illustrate this principle by teaching the Parable of the Unmerciful Servant. A certain king wanted to settle his accounts with his servants. One servant was brought to him who owed him ten thousand talents but who was unable to pay. The king in a fit of rage, commanded that the servant be sold along with his wife and children and possessions so as to settle the debt. The servant, overwhelmed with grief, fell down before the king and begged for mercy,

> *Master, have patience with me, and I will pay you all. Then the master of that servant was moved with compassion, released him, and forgave him the debt.*
>
> Matthew 18:26-27 (N.K.J.V.)

This servant who had received mercy from his master then went out and issued a dire threat to one of his fellow servants who owed him a small amount of money. He takes him by the throat demanding that he immediately settle this outstanding sum. The fellow servant was financially embarrassed and was in no position to settle the debt, and he begged for mercy from the one who had previously received such from his master.

An Unforgiving Spirit

> *Have patience with me, and I will pay you all, and he would not, but went out and threw him into prison till he should pay the debt.*
>
> Matthew 18:29-30 (N.K.J.V.)

When his fellow servants saw that the one who had been released from the large debt was unwilling to extend consideration to one who owed only a small debt, they were angry and reported him to his master. The offending servant was immediately summoned into the presence of the master and was forcibly reminded of the fact that mercy had been shown to him. He was asked to justify his actions,

> *Should you not also have had compassion on your fellow servant, just as I had pity on you?*
>
> Matthew 18:33 (N.K.J.V.)

The one who had received mercy should have in turn shown mercy, but instead he incurred the wrath of his master for his refusal to help his fellow servant. As punishment, he was delivered to the torturers until such time as he paid his debt in full.

The principle that Jesus is teaching here is simply this; the person who in his humility acknowledges that forgiveness has been

126

granted by a merciful God, will at all times seek to extend grace to those who may be the cause of offence. Failure to forgive those who sin against us will mean that God in turn will not forgive our sins and failures. Freely you have received, freely give.

"And Lead us not into Temptation"

We have already commented upon the warfare engaged in by every believer on a daily basis. There are times in which we can feel as though we are being overwhelmed by the attacks that come our way. Jesus exhorts His disciples with another petition; that they pray for strength to withstand this attack, and that they be protected from situations and circumstances which may place them in a position of vulnerability. The child of God needs constant reminding of the truth that God has delivered us from this present evil age, and has called us to walk before Him in the power of the Holy Spirit. Paul reminds his readers that they are not to make any provision for the flesh to fulfil its lusts, but there must be that determination to walk in the light as He (Jesus) is in the light. This petition has a very powerful application in our daily walk with God. Where the individual is conscious of an area of weakness in their life i.e. pornography, gambling, drug abuse etc., he or she must ensure that they stay clear of places, TV programmes, books and magazines that would activate and stimulate that weakness. God cannot do this for us, this has to be an act of the individual will coupled with the application of this petition in our prayer life. It is in this context that Jesus exhorts us to pray for deliverance from the snare of the evil one.

"For Yours is the Kingdom"

The prayer began with reference to the supreme greatness of God our Father. Jesus exhorts His disciples to at all times honour and revere His great Name. There follows that yearning for the full revelation of the Kingdom of God here on earth as in Heaven. The prayer then, as we have seen, takes the form of petitions that have to do with the daily necessities of life.

The prayer comes to a glorious climax by re-affirming the matchless power and authority of God. Believers pray this great prayer in the midst of a broken world inhabited by dysfunctional humanity, a world reserved for fire and destruction.

This closing statement reminds us of the bigger picture,

> *His is the Kingdom and the power and the glory,*
> *for ever, amen!*

In this manner, therefore pray.

Chapter 7

Intimacy with the Father

The High Priestly Prayer of Jesus
John 17

This great High Priestly prayer of Jesus has been referred to by many commentators as the "True Lord's Prayer." In our previous chapter we examined the prayer taught by Jesus to the disciples, a prayer that has been universally recognised as "The Lord's Prayer." However, it would be more accurate to regard the prayer of Jesus recorded in the gospels of Matthew and Luke as the "Model" prayer. Jesus taught it in response to the request made by the disciples, "Lord, teach us to pray." In this chapter we are going to look at two further prayers prayed by Jesus. Both prayers were prayed in moments of great passion as He looked ahead to the cross. The two prayers under discussion being His High Priestly prayer, and the prayer He prayed in the Garden of Gethsemane just prior to His arrest.

The High Priestly Prayer

There is a sense in which this majestic prayer should be approached with reverence and awe. John portrays moments of great intimacy between Jesus and the Father as they share in fellowship and communion just hours prior to Calvary. Not only does this passage reveal to us something of the relationship that existed between them, but it also illustrates the manner in which Jesus intercedes for believers in the presence of His Father. He engages in prayer on three levels; He prays for Himself, He prays for His disciples, and He prays for all believers, encompassing the church age from the Day of Pentecost up until the time of His second coming. The passion of this prayer is for the glory of God to be manifest, firstly in Himself as He seeks to be obedient to the will of His Father, secondly in the lives of His disciples, and lastly in the life and mission of the church.

1.   *Jesus Prays for Himself*
John 17:1-5

In speaking these words He lifted up His eyes to Heaven and said,

> *Father, the hour has come. Glorify your Son that*
> *your Son also may glorify you.*
>
> John 17:1 (N.K.J.V.)

This was one of the most poignant moments in the earthly life and ministry of Jesus. The cross of Calvary was not something that was suddenly thrust upon Him as some unexpected demand or obligation. Right from the beginning of His earthly ministry Jesus was fully aware of the purpose of His mission in that He

130

had come not to be served, but to serve, and to give His life as a ransom for many. As He begins this prayer, it would seem that His whole life up until that point was under review, all that He had sought to undertake by way of service and ministry dominated His thoughts. He is now fully aware that He is fast approaching the moment in which the real purpose of His mission is to be defined.

"The Hour has Come"

This the most important hour of human history. This was to be the hour in which the whole destiny of mankind was to be determined,

> *The hour has come that the Son of man should be glorified.*
>> John 12:23 (N.K.J.V.)

> *When Jesus knew that his hour had come that he should depart from this world to the Father.*
>> John 13:1 (N.K.J.V.)

a)   He Affirms the Glory of the Cross

As Jesus anticipates the cross, He is not regarding it as a moment of defeat in which His enemies were about to triumph over Him. Far from this, He affirms the glory and victory that the cross would bring in securing salvation for lost mankind,

> *Glorify Your Son, that your Son also may glorify you.*
>> John 17:1 (N.K.J.V.)

In the eyes of the world the cross was a spectacle of shame and humiliation, a form of death reserved for the most dangerous of criminals. There could never be any glory attached to such a barbaric act of cruelty, it was the most hideous of deaths. Nevertheless, the magnitude of Christ's sufferings could never obliterate the eternal glory that would be His as He put to flight Satan and his emissaries. His six hours on the cross, bearing as He did the guilt of broken humanity, the pain and suffering, the ridicule and taunts of the Roman soldiers, unquenchable thirst etc., constituted the most sublime act of obedience ever undertaken. This was His hour of glory in that He demonstrated absolute conformity to the will of the Father. The glory that Jesus prayed for was manifested three days later in His glorious resurrection from the dead. This was His Father's seal upon the great sacrifice made by His Son.

The motivation behind this request is so profound. Jesus was not seeking the glory of a martyr, or one dying for a worthy cause. His desire for glory was asked for on the basis that His Father in turn may be glorified.

b)   He Defines the Meaning of Eternal Life

His prayer at this point goes on to another level and deals with the subject of eternal life, a matter that really is the essence of salvation,

> *And this is life eternal, that they may know You,*
> *the only true God, and Jesus Christ whom You*
> *have sent.*
>
> John 17:3 (N.K.J.V.)

Enshrined in this prayer is the "Roadmap" to salvation. It can only be entered into as the seeker comes to an understanding of a Holy God, One who cannot entertain sin in any form, but One also who delights in mercy and compassion. It is not just "knowing" God, but it is a clear recognition that He is the "Only True God" and not one of a pantheon of gods. This is a message that must be preached with great power and conviction from our pulpits. There is widespread confusion in the hearts and minds of many people concerning the mixed signals coming from the church today particularly in the light of the whole "Multi-faith" agenda. Salvation can only be entered into through a clear understanding that Father God is "The only true God," and besides Him there is no other.

"And Jesus Christ whom You have Sent"

Jesus throughout His earthly ministry at all times sought to manifest the character and attributes of His Father. He was at pains to point out that He was undertaking this mission in response to the supreme will of His Father. To that end He had been "Sent" by the Father to declare the gospel of the Kingdom. Therefore eternal life can only be entered into through an understanding as to who God is, and that His manifest will and purpose has been defined through His Son, the Lord Jesus Christ.

Jesus Reviews His Mission

> *I have glorified You on the earth. I have finished the work You gave me to do.*
>
> John 17:4 (N.K.J.V.)

Jesus in praying this great High Priestly prayer is conducting a review of His ministry to date. He reflects upon His mighty works, His profound teaching, His interaction with people, His love and compassion, His stand for truth and righteousness etc. All of these aspects of ministry brought glory to the Father. He was not just thinking in terms of ministry and service to date, but He was also giving consideration to His impending death and resurrection, both of which would bring even greater glory to His Father. Jesus could truly claim that He had accomplished all required of Him in terms of declaring the gospel and that the task assigned Him was complete.

c)   *He Looks Ahead to a Renewal of Shared Glory*

> *And now, O Father, glorify me together with*
> *yourself, with the glory which I had with You*
> *before the world was.*
>
> John 17:5 (N.K.J.V.)

Prior to His incarnation, Jesus dwelt in the glories of Heaven with the Father, all of His deity displayed before the angelic host. When He came down amongst men He surrendered His heavenly glory in a supreme act of obedience to the will of the Father,

> *And being found in appearance as a man, He*
> *humbled Himself and became obedient to death,*
> *even the death of the cross.*
>
> Philippians 2:8 (N.K.J.V.)

Although Jesus was still God during His earthly ministry, this was not understood by the great majority of people; they regarded Him merely as the "Carpenter's Son" from lowly Nazareth. Now with His mission on the verge of completion, Jesus anticipates that renewed level of glory He shared with the Father prior to the foundation of the world. When we consider the words prayed by Jesus in this great prayer, we appreciate afresh the need to approach this with great humility and gratitude.

2.   *Jesus prays for His Disciples*

The prayer now changes direction as Jesus begins to pray for His disciples; the men that God had given Him out of the world. Jesus could truthfully say that He had declared the character and attributes of His Father to these men. He had spent three years pouring Himself into them and preparing them for the great task that lay ahead of them. Jesus had shared His heart with them, had put up with their repeated failings, enjoyed moments of leisure and relaxation with them, but He never claimed ownership of them. These were the men given to Him by the Father, they belonged to the Father and had kept the word given to them. As we examine this section of the High Priestly prayer of Jesus, we see clearly the great love and affection that compelled Him to pray for these men.

a)   *He Prays for their Knowledge*

The disciples had been with Jesus on His travels and had witnessed at first hand His mighty works. They had looked on as the ordinary people marvelled at the simplicity and clarity with which He taught. They overheard those who exclaimed; *"Never man spake like this man."* They had observed His authority over the forces of nature as He commanded the waves to be still. His exposure of the hypocrisy of the Scribes and Pharisees would have left an indelible imprint in their hearts and minds. Yet in all this, Jesus never sought to attract attention to Himself. He never craved the plaudits of men, He at all times was taken up with bringing glory to the Father.

Jesus made it abundantly clear to the disciples that He did not speak or act in accordance with His own authority, but only ministered in response to the directives given Him by His Father. This is clearly seen in the words contained in this great prayer,

> *For I have given to them the words which You have given me; and they have received them, and have known surely that I came forth from You; and they have believed that You sent me.*
>
> John 17:8 (N.K.J.V.)

b)   *He Prays for their Preservation*

The intimacy that existed between Jesus and the Father is clearly portrayed here,

> *All mine are Yours, and Yours are mine, and I am glorified in them.*
>
> John 17:10 (N.K.J.V.)

This section of the prayer also illustrates the perfect union that exists between Father and Son. Jesus is speaking in terms of "Co-ownership," equally shared between Father and Son, and He is doing so in the context of His disciples, all of whom were very ordinary men. The fact that they were just ordinary men did not influence Jesus in His choice of them, their humble background did not disqualify them from manifesting His glory and power. This remains the great desire in the heart of Jesus today that the church in all her expressions of ministry and service may seek to glorify her Lord and Saviour. Where ministry is motivated by a desire to promote His glory, blessing and increase will result. When it is exercised in praise of men, lasting fruit will be conspicuous by its absence. Jesus, in praying for their preservation, is mindful of the fact that His earthly sojourn is about to end, *"Now I am no longer in the world, but these are in the world."* He is praying for their preservation as they launch out in the great task of preaching the gospel to nations near and far,

> *Holy Father, keep through Your name those whom You have given me, that they may be one as we are one.*
>
> John 17:11 (N.K.J.V.)

In praying for His disciples, Jesus is mindful of the traumatic effect the events of the next few days would have upon them as they wrestled with the spectacle of His sufferings and death. He asked for the Father's keeping power to be upon them both in terms of their immediate future, but also with regard to the task awaiting them. In addition to praying for their preservation, Jesus prays for there to be a unity of purpose and vision in their ranks as they seek to implement the great commission to preach the gospel to all nations. The final statement in this prayer for their preservation makes reference to the fact that Jesus in His dealings with the disciples has kept them in and through the power of His Father's Name. Not one of them has been lost except the "Son of Perdition," a clear reference to Judas Iscariot who chose to betray His Lord and Master. This narrative contains some powerful truths for the church to take on board today. The church is in a state of constant warfare and she faces an enemy bent upon her destruction. Whilst we need to be mindful of the strategy of Satan and his forces, we are nevertheless reminded that greater is He that is in us than he that is in the world.

c) He Prays that they may Experience Joy

Jesus in praying this great prayer in the presence of His disciples, is demonstrating to them that this prayer, now being prayed before them, will continue to be prayed in the presence of His Father when He returns to Heaven,

> *But now I come to You, and these things I speak*
> *in the world, that they may have my joy fulfilled*
> *in themselves.*
>
> John 17:13 (N.K.J.V.)

Jesus looks ahead a short time following His resurrection and ascension to the events that were to happen on the Day of Pentecost as the Holy Spirit would be outpoured upon these men. Their mission would be fraught with danger, they would encounter stiff opposition, but their ministry would be accompanied by a great joy as they saw lives changed by the power of the gospel. The same is true for the church as she seeks to proclaim this wonderful message. Trials and adversity will most surely come, but Jesus is praying before the Father that joy may permeate the hearts of His servants as they remain faithful to the task in hand.

d) He Prays that they may be Set Apart

The actual term that Jesus uses here is "Sanctified," it means to "Set Apart." This process of sanctification would come at a cost in that they would be hated by the world on account of their dedication to the cause of the gospel,

*I have given them your word; and the world has
hated them because they are not of the world,
just as I am not of the world,*

John 17:14 (N.K.J.V.)

As the disciples received the Word of God and in turn began to display some of the characteristics of Jesus, the world would turn against them and hate them. The message of the gospel is at variance with the values of this world, and those who choose to live in accordance with its truth will find themselves targets for the world's ridicule and hatred. Jesus encountered this on repeated occasions in His earthly ministry particularly at the hands of the religious leaders of His day, but it did not deflect Him from the task given Him by His Father.

The church of Jesus Christ today in many parts of the world is facing great opposition with many believers paying the ultimate price of martyrdom for the sake of the gospel. This is symptomatic of the battle that rages between the Kingdom of God and the Kingdom of darkness. Jesus warns His followers that in the world they will face tribulation, but to be of good cheer, for He had overcome the world.

A Prayer to Stay the Course

*I do not pray that you should take them out of
the world, but that you should keep them from
the evil one.*

John 17:15 (N.K.J.V.)

It would be wrong for the believer to be taken out of the world. The church is called to be "in" the world but not "of" it. We are called to be "salt and light," to proclaim the great healing and reconciling message of the Kingdom of God. The prayer of Jesus is not for withdrawal, but for God's protection to all who would seek to live and witness for Him. The church must not only preach the gospel, but must also engage in the great social issues of the day. The voice of the church must be clearly heard in the corridors of power and influence. All disciples can be sure of God's keeping power as they seek to live for Him.

Jesus Prays "Set Them Apart" How?

> *Sanctify them by Your truth. Your word is truth.*
> John 17:17 (N.K.J.V.)

Jesus in praying for His disciples now asks the Father to set them apart for the mission to which they will be called. The word here is "Sanctify," it denotes a process that is about to take place in the hearts and lives of these men. Comment has already been made relative to their time spent with Jesus to date and how they will have observed at close quarters the methodology and style of His ministry. Now the time was fast approaching when they would be thrust out in the footsteps of their Lord and Master. Jesus is asking that these disciples may be those who would be set apart from the distractions of the world, and that their hearts and minds be focused on the task ahead. The most effective way in which this can be accomplished is through diligent study of the Word of God. Jesus here is referring to the powerful effect scripture has in guiding the steps of those who seek to serve.

This process is enhanced with the sure knowledge that His Word is the Word of "Truth." There needs to be a fresh determination on the part of believers today to immerse themselves in the truths of scripture. Church leaders need to take this on board. It is so very easy to regard the Bible as a "text book" from which we construct sermon material. This is a snare of the enemy and serves to rob us of the glorious power that is available as we allow the Holy Spirit to teach us and to guide us into all truth.

e)   *Jesus Prays for their Mission*

Jesus now prays for the future mission each one of His disciples would be called upon to undertake.

Divine Partnership

> *As You have sent me into the world, I also have sent them into the world.*
>
> John 17:18 (N.K.J.V.)

There can be no doubt that Jesus exercised His ministry in response to the directives of the Father. He was the "Sent One," sent by Father God to be the light of the world. Jesus now affirms the authority by which the mission of the church is to be conducted. The church is to take this gospel of the Kingdom to a lost world in response to the commission given her by her Lord and Saviour. In the same way that Jesus had been sent into the world by the Father, so these disciples would be sent in response to the mandate given by the Son.

This sending forth would commence with the outpouring of the Holy Spirit on the Day of Pentecost up until the time when Christ would return in glory to set up His Eternal Kingdom.

3.   *Jesus Prays for all Believers*

This great High Priestly Prayer of Jesus now extends to all who embrace the gospel through the witness and testimony of the

141

disciples. The ministry of the disciples post Pentecost laid the foundation for what we have come to understand as the Church Age. There are two specifics contained in this section of the prayer: firstly, that there may be unity in heart and mind, secondly; that all believers might share His Heavenly glory.

a) *He Prays for Unity*

Jesus in praying this has in mind the great task assigned to the church in her quest to preach the gospel to all nations. This was to be a monumental undertaking given the fearsome opposition the mission would attract. Unity would be a major key in the advancement of their cause, failure in this vital area of church life would only serve to dissipate their energies and limit the impact of their message. The unity that Jesus prays for is not just for the purpose of cohesion and expansion, but it is unity that would announce to a broken world that Jesus had been sent by Father God to redeem mankind from the power of sin.

This is such an important principle to bear in mind today as we seek to advance the testimony of the church. Any outward form of disunity will not only reflect badly upon the church, but will only serve to undermine her mission and calling. How can believers minister grace to a fractured society when there is disunity and discord within. More damage is done to the reputation of the church by disunity than by any other single factor. This is clearly a concern in the heart of Jesus as He makes this petition to His Father.

The unity of the disciples is not just simply a unity that needs to find expression within their ranks, it is a unity that is so powerfully at work within the framework of the Trinity,

And the glory which you gave me I have given
them, that they may be one just as we are one.

John 17:22 (N.K.J.V.)

What is the Nature of this Unity?

Jesus is not praying for the imposition of some artificial unified church structure the like of which has been attempted in recent decades, His prayer goes much deeper than that. He is praying for a unity to be evidenced as the church fulfils her mission in declaring the greatness, the power, and the love of God. This unity cannot be institutional, it must be relational, and it must be outworked at heart level. It is a unity that is forged when believers recognise the supreme priority of the church as being that of mission, reaching out to a lost world.

Another important factor that must be remembered here is that the unity for which Christ prays can only be outworked upon the basis of the revealed truth of scripture. Any deviation from this, any attempt to express unity from any other base than the truth of scripture is doomed to failure and is a denial of the petition prayed by Jesus in verse seventeen,

Sanctify them by Your truth, Your word is truth.

John 17:17 (N.K.J.V.)

Unity and Glory

At the beginning of the prayer, Jesus speaks in terms of the glory bestowed on Him by the Father. The passion of Jesus is for this same glory to be shared with all believers thus establishing the unbreakable link that exists between unity and glory. The glory of the church is that she is united in Christ, equipped and empowered to declare the message of the gospel to a dying world.

b)   *He Prays for their Future Fellowship with Him*

Jesus prays for the future presence of believers with Him in glory,

> *Father, I desire that they also whom you gave*
> *me may be with me where I am, that they may*
> *behold my glory which you have given me.*
>
> John 17:24 (N.K.J.V.)

He is referring to the eternal state of all who belong to Him. This request is answered at the death of each dear saint who has made their peace with Father God. For the Christian there is no fear in death. The physical body may cease to function, but there is that immediate entrance into the presence of the Lord Jesus. In praying in this manner, Jesus is again stating the extent of His love toward His Body, the church. As He utters this petition He is only hours away from the cross, it is therefore a request that not only refers to the security of the child of God, but it is for Jesus a factor that brings great comfort to Himself as He looks ahead to the fellowship in glory with His saints.

c)   *He Prays for their Abiding Love*

> *And I have declared to them your name, and will*
> *declare it, that the love with which You loved me*
> *may be in them, and I in them.*
>
> John 17:26 (N.K.J.V.)

This great High Priestly prayer of Jesus now comes to a powerful climax. He looks back for a moment on His mission and reflects upon the way in which He has declared the Father's Name to the disciples. He had made it abundantly clear to them on a number of occasions that the words and the works He did were not His own, but were the words and works of the Father. The disciples had seen in Jesus an exact representation of all that the Father was both in terms of His character and attributes.

This declaration of the Father's Name would continue in and through the ministry of the church beginning at the Day of Pentecost right up to the end of the age.

Declaring the Father's Love

> *That the love with which you loved me may be in them, and I in them.*
>
> John 17:26 (N.K.J.V.)

This final statement of Jesus should serve as a powerful incentive for every Christian to remain faithful to Him and to the cause of His Kingdom. One cannot even begin to fathom the depth of love the Father bestowed upon His Son, our minds just simply cannot comprehend the sheer magnitude of such love. Jesus here is praying that the love expressed by the Father toward Him as His Son may also be directed toward each and every believer. This has been made possible through Christ's atoning work on the cross. Christ's death takes the form of a dramatic statement made by Father God. It is a statement declaring His love toward sinful man, a love expressed in tangible form by the gift of His Son Jesus to die in our place,

But God demonstrates His own love toward us,
in that while we were still sinners, Christ died
for us.

Romans 5:8 (N.K.J.V.)

At the point of salvation, as the sinner comes to faith in Christ, he or she is immediately indwelt by the Holy Spirit. Something of the nature of Christ is implanted within, it is therefore on this basis that God is able to declare His great love toward all believers,

So that Your love for me might be in them
exactly as I am in them.

(The Message)

Conclusion

As Jesus prayed this prayer, just hours prior to the cross, there were three factors that motivated Him; mission, faithfulness, and unity. He prays for the glory of God to be seen in the granting of eternal life to the penitent. He prays for the preservation and perseverance of His people as they proclaim the gospel to a hostile world. He prays that all believers may experience that unity of the Spirit that is so essential to the completion of their call to preach the gospel to all nations.

The Prayer of Jesus in Gethsemane
Matthew 26

We have looked at two of the prayers prayed by Jesus in public; namely the "Model" prayer He taught His disciples, and the "High Priestly" prayer recorded in the 17th chapter of John. We are going to conclude this chapter by examining the incredible prayer of Jesus prayed in the Garden of Gethsemane just hours before going to the cross.

The contrast between this prayer and His "High Priestly" prayer cannot be more stark. The majestic cadences of John 17 give way to the passionate heartcry and distress of the Gethsemane scene. We see Jesus at just about the lowest point of His earthly mission. The most bitter cup of all is about to be drunk as He contemplates His role as mankind's sin bearer.

Setting the Scene

Jesus had just instituted the Lord's Supper with His disciples, this was followed by His prediction of Peter's denial. He now arrives at the Garden of Gethsemane accompanied by Peter and the two sons of Zebedee,

> *Then He said to them, my soul is exceedingly sorrowful, even to death. Stay here and watch with me.*
>
> Matthew 26:38 (N.K.J.V.)

Gethsemane – Oil Press
"A place of crushing"

The meaning of the place name accurately described what Jesus was about to endure. For Him this was to be a place in which He would indeed be pressed and crushed. This was Satan's moment, it was the hour he had been waiting for, the moment in which he and his forces were bent upon the final destruction of Jesus, and with His destruction any possibility of redeeming lost mankind.

A Pivotal Moment

> *He went a little farther and fell on his face, and prayed, saying, O my Father, if it be possible, let this cup pass from me; nevertheless, not as I will, but as You will.*
>
> Matthew 26:39 (N.K.J.V.)

The "Cup" in the Old Testament is a metaphor signifying Divine punishment for sin. Jesus in praying this prayer was giving expression to His understanding of the sequence of events that were about to unfold. He clearly understood that His death was not just a physical death, as cruel as that was to be, at the hands of barbaric Roman soldiers, but in addition to that, He was to become the object of Divine wrath as He took upon Himself the guilt of sinful man,

> *For He made Him who knew no sin to be sin for us, that we might become the righteousness of God in Him.*
>
> 2 Corinthians 5:21 (N.K.J.V.)

> *And the Lord has laid upon Him the iniquity of us all.*
>
> Isaiah 53:6 (N.K.J.V.)

"Let this Cup Pass from Me"

It must be stressed here that this request of Jesus did not momentarily constitute a refusal to go through with His sufferings as some have suggested, this would be contrary to His statement of intent recorded in the John 12,

Now my soul is troubled, and what shall I say?
Father save me from this hour? But for this
purpose I came to this hour.

John 12:27 (N.K.J.V.)

The issue is not one of submitting to the will of His Father, but whether this entailed the spectacle of this cruel cup. In other words, could there be another way by which to secure the salvation of sinners other than by the way of the cross? If so, let it be made known now. Even in the midst of this great agony of heart Jesus in no way, even for a split second, sought to usurp the will of His Father.

"Sweat Drops of Blood"

Luke makes mention of this extreme condition manifested by Jesus. Luke describes in graphic detail the agony experienced by Jesus as He cried to His Father. However, even in the midst of this crushing, He did not turn His back from the task that awaited Him.

Jesus momentarily left the scene and returned to His disciples and found them sleeping. Such was their distress and confusion they could not find it within themselves to watch and pray just for one hour. Jesus returns to the garden a second time and again prays this agonising prayer and in so doing expressed total submission to the will of His Father.

Having been to the place of "Crushing," and having gone through extreme depths of sorrow, Jesus now moves on from that scene ready to face what was ahead of Him. Far from Him stepping back from this hour of trial, Jesus went forward with determination ready to do all that He had to do in order to secure freedom for sinful man.

Rise, let us be going...

Chapter 8

Jesus – Prayer and Boldness

We are going to devote one more chapter to looking at aspects of prayer in the life and ministry of Jesus. Reference has already been made concerning the importance Jesus attached to prayer. The gospel writers portray Him at prayer both before and after seasons of ministry. For Jesus, communion with His Father was a matter of prime importance. It was during such times that Jesus had revealed to Him the nature of the work He was to undertake in His task of preaching the gospel of the Kingdom. The purpose of this chapter is to examine the teaching of Jesus relative to "boldness" in prayer, and to look at instances in which boldness was used by various people in their dealings with Him.

In chapter three we looked at the subject of "persistence" in prayer focusing on incidents in the lives of Abraham and Jacob. Persistence and boldness can be very closely related within the framework of prayer, and it is an aspect of prayer that was very much in evidence both in the life and teaching of Jesus. It must be said that one of the great deficiencies in the devotional life of the individual believer, and also in the corporate life of the church, is the lack of boldness and perseverance in relation to prayer. So very often our efforts can be weak and insipid, lacking focus and direction. This is a matter that needs to be urgently addressed if the church is going to respond to the challenge of the hour.

Jesus identified the danger of weak and ineffective praying, He sought to correct it through the teaching of two parables, both recorded in the gospel of Luke; the parable of "The Persistent Friend," and the parable of "The Persistent Widow." The older translations of the scripture use the word; *"importunate"* in defining boldness in prayer, it may help to establish a definition:

Importunate
"persistent pressing"

It comes from the Latin word "importunas" and suggests an approach that is both troublesome or inconvenient. The Greek rendering is the word "shamelessness," suggesting a determination on the part of the petitioner to press through with the matter in hand. It is this dimension of boldness that Jesus is calling for in terms of the way in which we approach this aspect of prayer.

The Parable of the "Importunate" Friend
Luke 11

This passage illustrates very powerfully the need for boldness in the way in which we engage in prayer. It immediately follows the "model" prayer taught by Jesus to His disciples in response to their request that He teach them to pray. Having given this framework, Jesus now proceeds to lay great emphasis on the importance of perseverance and boldness in prayer. This story has been regarded by some as the "Parable of the Friend at Midnight." There are three central characters to this story; there is the visiting friend, the importunate friend, and the unwilling friend. Jesus, in adopting this method of teaching, draws upon the cultural norm of the day in respect of hospitality.

In Biblical times, hospitality to strangers was looked upon as a matter of prime importance. A typical Jewish household would always seek to be ready for the most unexpected eventuality, even the prospect of providing food and shelter late into the night. In addition to this, it was a cultural norm for neighbours to borrow from each other should the need arise. It was regarded as a social disaster for a traveller to be refused the most basic provision of hospitality, and it would almost take the form of a social stigma to refuse such a request.

a) *The Visiting Friend*

Here we have a tired and hungry traveller journeying at night so as to avoid the intense heat of the daytime. This was a practice that was a regular feature of travel in Biblical times. His journey led him to the vicinity of a close friend, and so in keeping with normal Jewish custom, he decided to call asking his friend for a meal and somewhere to sleep.

b) *The Importunate (persistent) Friend*

He heard the sound of the door knocking at the midnight hour and went to investigate who it was looking to speak to him at that late hour. To his surprise his friend whom he had not seen for some time was standing at the door requesting food and shelter. This was not an unreasonable request given the cultural norm of the day. Unfortunately the host was totally unprepared for this visit

153

and found himself in an acutely embarrassing situation in that his food cupboard was empty, not even a loaf of bread.

Jesus uses the plight of the embarrassed host in order to illustrate the need for boldness and perseverance in prayer,

> *And He said to them, which of you shall have a friend, and go to him at midnight and say to him, friend, lend me three loaves; for a friend of mine has come to me on his journey, and I have nothing to set before him.*
>
> Luke 11:5-6 (N.K.J.V.)

Such was his determination to provide the traveller with food and in so doing avoid maximum embarrassment, he thought nothing of awaking his neighbour and banging his door at midnight in order to borrow three loaves. There was a pressing need that required immediate action, and therefore he was not afraid to engage in this act of boldness even at the risk of annoying his neighbour. As the story unfolds, we see clearly illustrated the need for this level of perseverance to be manifest in our praying. The response the persistent friend received was not what he was hoping for.

c) *The Unwilling Friend*

> *And he will answer from within and say, do not trouble me; the door is now shut, and my children are with me in bed; I cannot rise and give to you.*
>
> Luke 11:7 (N.K.J.V.)

The embarrassed host was immediately met with an obstacle that threatened his reputation as an honourable member of that community. His request was met with a blank refusal that only served to add to his acute shame. The unwilling friend did not want to be troubled, his door was firmly shut, and his children were asleep in bed, it was midnight and his request was met with a polite but firm "No!"

This called for boldness and perseverance on the part of the embarrassed host, he would not be deflected from his quest to provide food for his unexpected guest, and therefore sought to overcome this barrier.

Boldness

> *I say to you, though he will not rise and give to him because he is his friend, yet because of his persistence he will rise and give him as many as he needs.*
>
> Luke 11:8 (N.K.J.V.)

The unwilling friend could not ignore the persistent knocking of his door and the importunate pleas of the embarrassed host. Not only did his refusal to help risk disturbing the sleep of his children, but there was a very strong possibility that the entire neighbourhood would be awakened by the persistent knocking.

The unwilling friend did eventually respond to the request for bread, but his response was not motivated through friendship, but it was made in the face of the boldness and persistence of the one asking for bread.

Importunity – Shamelessness

The embarrassed host in his determination to secure bread never once thought in terms of shame or disgrace, his sole motivation was the provision of a meal to the traveller.

Having taught the parable, Jesus proceeds to give the application in regard to boldness in prayer,

> *So I say to you, ask, and it will be given you; seek, and you will find; knock, and it will be opened to you.*
>
> Luke 11:9 (N.K.J.V.)

In teaching this parable, Jesus is illustrating the difference between the unwilling neighbour who eventually responded in a reluctant manner, to the grace and provision of Father God who delights to minister to the needs of His children day and night. If the unwilling friend responded in this fashion, how much more will God respond to the bold and determined cries of His people.

Boldness rewarded

> *For everyone who asks receives, and he who seeks finds, and to him who knocks it will be opened.*
>
> Luke 11:10 (N.K.J.V.)

Jesus in giving this Parable was not seeking to give the impression that God has to be badgered and coerced into answering our prayers. We do not force God to act, He can never stand accused of being a reluctant giver, but He will meet our request in accordance with His sovereign will and purpose, and in step with His perfect timing. The act of asking, seeking, and knocking is not God dangling petitioners on the end of a piece of string, it is an approach designed to strengthen our faith in His power and provision.

The Heart of God Revealed

Here Jesus demonstrates the manner in which Father God responds to the prayers of His people. He draws comparison with the motives and intentions of earthly fathers,

> *If a son asks for bread from any father among you, will he give him a stone? Or if he asks for a fish, will he give him a serpent instead of a fish? Or if he asks for an egg, will he give him a scorpion? If you then being evil, know how to give good gifts to your children, how much more will your Heavenly Father give the Holy Spirit to those who ask him?*
>
> Luke 11:11-13 (N.K.J.V.)

No normal earthly father would contemplate for a split second treating his children in the manner Jesus suggests. Even allowing for the bias toward evil that exists in every human heart, no father would seek to harm his child in a deliberate way. This being the case, how much more will our Father in heaven respond to the petitions and prayers of His people.

Good Gifts

> *Every good and perfect gift is from above, and comes down from the father of lights, with whom there is no variation or shadow of turning.*
>
> James 1:17 (N.K.J.V.)

This parable exhorts us not to grow weary in making our petitions known to God. Paul exhorts us to do so with thanksgiving.

Prayer and boldness: the parable of the unjust judge
Luke 18: 1 – 8

This parable along with the parable we have just examined, teaches the importance of bold and persevering prayer. Right from the beginning of this narrative Jesus comes straight to the point,

> *Then He spake a parable to them, that men ought always to pray and not to lose heart.*
>
> Luke 18:1-8 (N.K.J.V.)

So many believers lose heart and become discouraged through what they perceive to be unanswered prayer. This is particularly the case if prayer has been entered into with great fervency and integrity. There is that initial motivation to pray on the basis of felt need and the passionate desire to see God intervene. This level of praying then begins to diminish as weariness sets in along with resignation on the part of the petitioner that somehow God is refusing to respond to the cry from the heart. The next stage is that our prayers grind to a halt as we wrestle with the twin emotions of defeat and disappointment. It is exactly with this set of circumstances in mind that Jesus gives us the exhortation in this first verse,

> *Men ought always to pray and not to lose heart.*

Jesus here is calling for our prayer to be offered on a "continual" basis and not at a moment's notice as we seek to get God to respond to our timing and convenience. He is also teaching here that our prayers need to be specific as in the case of the widow in this Parable of the Unjust Judge.

So much power is lost in prayer through a failure to be specific. Our prayers need to be focused and delivered with passion and conviction. Jesus, as in the previous parable, uses three central characters to illustrate the need for boldness in the approach to prayer. The three characters being; the persevering widow, the unjust judge, and the righteous judge.

a) *The persevering (importunate) widow*

> *Now there was a widow in that city; and she came to him; (unjust judge), saying, get justice for me from my adversary.*
>
> Luke 18:3 (N.K.J.V.)

Here was a woman in a desperate situation who was clearly seeking justice. In Biblical times widows were a seriously disadvantaged sector of society. They were often left destitute following the death of their husbands, they were despised, and very often the prey for unscrupulous moneylenders. This widow has obviously been conned out of a sum of money and was seeking justice which was hers by right. Her plight was compounded by the fact that the judge appointed to hear her case was a hard and uncaring man who had no compassion for this poor woman. Although weighed down by her adverse circumstances, she was determined in the face of overwhelming odds to see that justice be dispensed on a fair and equitable basis. Far from being put off by the callous attitude of the uncaring judge, she persisted in her quest for justice.

b) *The unjust judge*

> *There was in a certain city a judge who did not fear God or respect man.*
>
> *Luke 18:2 (N.K.J.V.)*

Historical evidence tells us how the justice system that prevailed in Galilee was open to corruption and all kinds of mal-practice. This judge was possibly one of many whose only desire was to extort money out of weak and disadvantaged people such as this widow. However, this judge met his match in the form of this fighter of a woman who demonstrated great determination and boldness in her quest for justice.

After a period of time, the judge became weary with the constant demands of this widow, and he arrived at the point at which his patience was exhausted, and so he sought to find a way in which this matter could be settled.

The results of her boldness

> *...Afterward he said within himself, though I do not fear God nor regard man, yet because this widow troubles me I will vindicate her, lest by her continual coming she weary me.*
>
> Luke 18:4-5 (N.K.J.V.)

He had just about had enough of the constant petitioning of the widow, and for the sake of his peace of mind he decides to act. It is interesting to note the literal meaning of some of the terms employed by Jesus in the telling of this parable,

"Weary me" – "To wear out, to come to blows, to strike under the eyes!"

A literal translation could be, "To come to blows and give me a pair of black eyes!"

This judge did not administer justice in terms of equity and fairness, he only dealt with this case in order to escape from her constant lobbying.

c) *The righteous judge*

> *And shall God not avenge His own elect who cry out day and night to Him, though He bears long with them?*
>
> Luke 18:7 (N.K.J.V.)

The contrast between the unjust judge and the righteous judge cannot be more marked. We have seen how the unjust judge would only act with great reluctance toward the plight of the widow. This is in stark contrast with the grace and favour manifested by Father God in His response to the cries of His people. If the unjust judge responded only to rid himself of the constant pressure exerted by the boldness of the widow, how much more will our Heavenly Father, the "Righteous Judge" hear the prayers of His people that ascend to Him night and day?

If the boldness and perseverance of a widow won the day against the unjust judge, how much more will the rewards be for those who petition God on the basis of His love and grace? Jesus, knowing the heart of the Father, exhorts us to continue in prayer and not to be overcome by discouragement.

There may be times in which God's response is delayed. We must not immediately come to the conclusion that He is saying "No," He may be saying, "Not yet!" In responding to God's delays we must firstly remind ourselves that He has heard our prayer and will always act in accordance with His perfect will and purpose. Delays may serve to strengthen our faith as we wait upon Him knowing that He, as the "Judge of all the Earth" will always do right. We can also be assured that He is only concerned for our well being, and will preserve us from those things that will harm us or rob us of the intimacy that He so greatly desires. The Psalmist, in reflecting upon God's provision and timing, points the way forward and the path every believer should walk,

Commit your way to the Lord, trust also in Him, and He shall bring it to pass.
Psalm 37:5 (N.K.J.V.)

Prayer and Boldness
Practical Examples

We have examined these two parables that clearly illustrate the need for boldness and perseverance in our praying. We now take this a stage further by looking at some instances in the ministry of Jesus in which people approached Him, boldly requesting Him to demonstrate His power on their behalf.

The Syro-Phoenician Woman
Matthew 15

Here we have one of the most remarkable examples of persevering prayer found in the gospels. Jesus had been preaching in Galilee and had just completed an intense period of ministry reasoning with the Scribes and Pharisees. He leaves Galilee and departs to the region of Tyre and Sidon, a locality off limits to the normal location of His ministry. Matthew relates a most amazing incident in which Jesus is confronted by a Canaanite woman who cries to Him on behalf of her daughter who was severely demonised. Her approach to Jesus, requesting His intervention, seemed doomed to failure on the grounds that she was a Gentile and the ministry of Jesus at that point was strictly within the boundaries of Israel. Not only was she a Gentile, but she came from a nation that had been under the curse of God.

The political and religious constraints of this situation did not in any way deter this lady from boldly approaching Jesus requesting Him to heal her daughter.

The Request

> *A woman of Canaan came from that region and cried out to Him, saying, have mercy on me, O Lord, Son of David! My daughter is severely demonised.*
>
> Matthew 15:22 (N.K.J.V.)

She was well aware that the geographical location was outside of the boundaries of Christ's ministry, but this was balanced by the fact that she clearly understood who Jesus was in that she addressed Him as the "Son of David". Her boldness is demonstrated in the fact that she "cried out," nothing was going to stand in the way of securing help for her daughter, not least political or religious constraints. Her religious pedigree did not blind her to the fact that she was approaching Jesus as the "master healer", the only person who could meet this desperate need.

The immediate response of Jesus seemed to be so cruel in that He appeared to virtually ignore her. In addition to the seeming indifference shown by Jesus, the disciples were clearly annoyed by her persistence and were on the point of telling her to go away. In spite of this initial setback, the woman became even more determined in her approach to Jesus. If anything, the conduct of Jesus only served to stiffen her resolve and to increase her level of boldness. Eventually her dogged persistence elicits a response from Jesus, a response that hardly caused her hopes to rise,

> *...I was not sent except to the lost sheep of the house of Israel.*
> Matthew 15:24 (N.K.J.V.)

These words of Jesus could have crushed her spirit. She may have reasoned within herself that this man, the one who had been the great healer, the one who had always ministered from a great heart of compassion, and the one who had on a previous occasion healed a multitude of people which included many from her region, was now coldly rejecting her in a time of crisis. Far from being deterred, her boldness was raised to a higher level. She responded to this statement of Jesus by bowing before Him in an act of worship and again implored Him to intervene on behalf of her demonised daughter.

Jesus responds to this by making a further statement that could have been misconstrued as politically and religiously offensive in nature, but it was a statement designed to test the faith of the woman,

> *But He answered and said, it is not good to take the children's bread and throw it to the little dogs.*
> Matthew 15:26 (N.K.J.V.)

Jesus is here making reference to her status as a Gentile. His mission was essentially to the Jews. He had come to give the "children's bread" to the nation of Israel and this woman was clearly outside that circle. In using the term "dogs", He was also referring to the pejorative phrase used by the Jews, who in their disdain for the Gentiles, referred to them as "dogs".

Most people by now would have turned away from Jesus greatly offended by His seeming disregard for this woman's plight, but not this Syro-Phoenician lady, she was embued with a boldness and a determination that was driving her to press on in her dialogue with Jesus. There were two powerful motivating factors in play here that compelled her to persevere in her quest for healing. Firstly, she was motivated by her simple faith in the power of Jesus in spite of His apparent reluctance to get involved, and secondly, the condition of her daughter back at home, gripped by the power of an evil spirit. These two factors not only caused her to be bold in her approach to Jesus, but they also served to strengthen her faith in the face of what appeared to be huge barriers.

There follows an amazing statement on the part of the woman that clearly demonstrated her boldness and faith,

> *And she said, "Yes, Lord, yet even the little dogs eat the crumbs which fall from the Master's table."*
>
> Matthew 15:27 (N.K.J.V.)

She knew perfectly well that Jesus was not treating her with disdain, she had understood the nature of His mission in that it was primarily a mission to the Jews, but she did not allow these factors to in any way diminish her faith and trust in His mighty power. Her faith overcame political and religious barriers, and it was a faith that drew an immediate response from Jesus,

> *...O woman, great is your faith! Let it be to you as you desire. And her daughter was healed from that very hour.*
>
> Matthew 15:28 (N.K.J.V.)

Faith and Boldness

Boldness will always act as a vehicle by which faith can be strengthened. The approach of this Syro-Phoenician woman to Jesus provides a powerful illustration of how prayer can be energised by the application of these two forces.

The Healing of the Leper
Mark 1

Our purpose in looking at these mighty miracles in the ministry of Jesus is to see clearly the role that boldness in prayer played in the manifestation of His power. Jesus had been teaching in the synagogue in Capernaum and His teaching caused great astonishment among the people as He taught with authority in contrast to the weak insipid teaching coming from the Pharisees. His teaching was accompanied by mighty acts of healing and deliverance as the sick and demonised were restored. Following this ministry at Capernaum, Jesus moved on to teach in the synagogues throughout Galilee. It was on one such occasion that Jesus was confronted by a leper, who in an act of great boldness, knelt before Him, imploring Him to cleanse him of his leprosy.

Boldness

> Now a leper came to Him, imploring Him, kneeling down to Him and saying to Him, "if you are willing, you can make me clean."
>
> Mark 1:40 (N.K.J.V.)

This act of boldness on the part of the leper not only had political and religious implications, but also had much to do with his social status. In Biblical times, a leper was often regarded as one suffering on account of some sin, committed either by himself or one of his forebears. Jews often referred to leprosy as the "Finger of God" or "The Stroke". For the victim of this cruel disease it meant a life of misery in that he would have to live in isolation from the community, he would have to wear a placard bearing the message, "Unclean, unclean", and he would have to give warning to anyone approaching. In addition to this the sufferer was pronounced ritually unclean under the terms of Mosaic Law. Having understood this, we can see that it required great courage and boldness on the part of the leper to even think in terms of approaching Jesus!

The response of Jesus

> *Then Jesus, moved with compassion, stretched out*
> *His hand and touched him, and said to him, "I am*
> *willing; be cleansed."*
> Mark 1:41 (N.K.J.V.)

The boldness of the leper was no doubt driven by the reports that were circulating concerning the mighty works of Jesus. His simple faith provided him with the platform he needed to approach Jesus requesting healing from his leprosy. In response to the cry of this poor leper, Jesus did something unthinkable given the contagious nature of this disease – He touched him. Not only did Jesus touch him, but He ministered to him out of a heart of great compassion. The boldness of the leper not only activated the power of Jesus, but also His compassion. It is so important to note that Jesus demonstrated power and compassion in equal measure, and this must serve as a clear indicator to the church in the conducting of her mission to a needy world today.

The leper's boldness in the face of his extreme circumstances was to bear fruit as he heard the wonderful words of the Master,

"I am willing; be cleansed!"

Let us pause for a moment and seek to put ourselves in the position of this leper. Try to imagine the emotions and feelings that must have come to the fore as Jesus responded to his plight. This was the moment in which he experienced the mighty healing power of Jesus. From this point, his life would be totally transformed, he would be able to rejoin the community and play his role as an honourable citizen of that town.

The Cure

> As soon as He had spoken, immediately the leprosy left him, and he was cleansed.
>
> Mark 1:42 (N.K.J.V.)

The bold contact made by the leper and the word of command spoken by Jesus, resulted in a complete and lasting cure for this man who otherwise would have been the victim of a slow and miserable death.

Blind Bartimaeus
Mark 10

There are several other instances recorded in the gospels in which we see people approaching Jesus with boldness in respect of their needs. One of the most powerful is Mark 10 concerning blind Bartimaeus.

Jesus is passing through the city of Jericho with His disciples accompanied by a great multitude of people. There was a sense of great excitement in the city as the crowds thronged to see Jesus. Reports were to hand concerning the amazing miracles He had performed. Crowds gathered on the pavements in eager anticipation seeking to gain vantage points from which they might just catch a glimpse of the Master. One can imagine scenes of great joy as children were hoisted onto the shoulders of their parents so that they too could see this very special visitor to their city.

In the midst of this swelling crowd, there sat a man for whom this day was to signal a change in the entire course of his life,

> *...blind Bartimaeus, the son of Timaeus, sat by the road begging.*
>
> Mark 10:46 (N.K.J.V.)

This poor man lived an existence of penury. He was well known in the community in that he would be seen begging by the roadside every day of the week. Many would have looked upon him merely as a vagrant, an unwelcome sight in the city centre of Jericho, however, begging was the only means at his disposal with which to survive.

Although Bartimaeus was blind, he could tell that something was about to happen as the people began to fill the streets and the pavements. He tried to catch some of the conversation of the crowds to see if he could find out the reason for this high level of excitement. He then heard the name of Jesus mentioned and soon realised that it was He who was about to pass through Jericho that day.

The impact of this was immediate for Bartimaeus. He had heard much talk about this man Jesus, and had heard reports of the mighty works of healing that were taking place, including the opening of blind eyes. Something inside Bartimaeus registered, he reasoned that Jesus had the power to open blind eyes, and that it was He who was about to pass his way today. Bartimaeus knew that his blindness placed him at a disadvantage in terms of attracting the attention of Jesus, but this would not deter him in his quest. He began to manifest the same degree of boldness in approaching Jesus as the boldness employed by the Syro-Phoenician woman and the leper.

Prayer and Boldness

> *And when he heard that it was Jesus of Nazareth, he began to cry out and say, "Jesus, son of David, have mercy on me."*
>
> Mark 10:47 (N.K.J.V.)

Bartimaeus may have been blind and destitute, but he possessed a keen understanding as to the identity of Jesus in that he addressed Him as *"Jesus of Nazareth – Son of David"*. Bartimaeus in his approach to Jesus was boldly declaring that his faith and trust was in His person and power.

The Response of the Crowd

> *Then many warned him to be quiet; but he cried out all the more, "Son of David, have mercy on me!"*
>
> Mark 10:48 (N.K.J.V.)

Not only did Bartimaeus have to contend with the fact that he was just a mere blind beggar, but his cries offended the civic pride of many who had gathered. They wanted Jesus to obtain a favourable impression of their city and they did not want this put at risk by the rantings of this vagrant. Their attempts to silence him failed as Jesus looked in his direction.

Boldness Rewarded

> *So Jesus stood still and commanded him to be called. Then they called the blind man, saying to him, "be of good cheer. Rise, He is calling you."*
> Mark 10:49 (N.K.J.V.)

Bartimaeus immediately threw aside his tattered garment and came before Jesus, his heart beating with nervous expectancy. Jesus then asked him a question,

"What do you want me to do for you?"

In a statement of powerful simplicity and trust, Bartimaeus replied,

"Teacher, that I may receive my sight."

The thronging crowds looked on in wonder and amazement as this beggar, who they knew to be the same man who sat begging in the city centre on a daily basis, was engaged in conversation with Jesus. The gathered crowd failed to realise that it was for people such as blind Bartimaeus that Jesus had come to minister. This day belonged to Bartimaeus and no one was going to take that away from him.

The Result

> *Then Jesus said to him, "Go your way; your faith has made you whole." And immediately he received his sight and followed Jesus on the road.*
>
> Mark 10:52 (N.K.J.V.)

Conclusion

The Syro-Phoenician woman, the leper and blind Bartimaeus in their dealings with Jesus demonstrated the power that is available in response to boldness in prayer!

Men ought always to pray and not to lose heart!

Chapter 9

The Promise Of The Holy Spirit

Here I am, walking through a crowded shopping centre in one of our largest cities, when I notice the person with the proverbial clipboard and pen walking in my direction eagerly awaiting my response to a range of questions. He was a student from a local college, and as part of his "Humanities" course, he was conducting a street survey seeking the views of people concerning the role of the church in 21st century Britain. One of the questions on the survey had to do with the whole issue of Christianity and the "Post-Modern" mindset of our day. When he discovered that I was an ordained minister and that I was more than willing to answer his questions, his whole approach dramatically changed. Following my meeting with this student, I began to reflect upon the exercise I had just been part of. I thought for some time about the impact this survey would have upon that young man and his fellow students who were conducting similar surveys in other parts of the city centre. I found myself asking the simple question, "What role has the church to fulfil in 21st century Britain?"

The role of the church has and always will be the same and does not change with the passing of time, nor is that role influenced by the cultural values of the age. The church has been commissioned to be the vehicle through which the gospel of the Kingdom of God is proclaimed. Her calling is to be faithful to "The Great Commission" given her by Jesus Christ,

> *All authority has been given to Me in heaven and on earth. Go, therefore, and make disciples of all the nations, baptising them in the name of the Father and of the Son and of the Holy Spirit, teaching them to observe all things that I have commanded you; and lo, I am with you always, even to the end of the age. Amen.*
>
> Matthew 28:18-20 (N.K.J.V.)

This was the mandate given by Jesus to His disciples just prior to His ascension and is repeated with a slight variation in the gospels of Mark and Luke.

The Promise of the Holy Spirit

There is an unbreakable link between prayer and the outpouring of the Holy Spirit, particularly in relation to the mission of the church. It is impossible to separate these two great forces, they combine to empower and direct the proclamation of the good news of the gospel. The bold declaration of the gospel, when undertaken in the power of the Holy Spirit and in response to prevailing prayer, will result in transformed lives and communities. There are nations around the globe today that are experiencing powerful moves of the Holy Spirit resulting in multitudes coming to faith in Christ. Where this is happening, prayer is seen to be the key through which God's power is released. New churches are being birthed, and existing congregations are experiencing renewal, as believers re-discover the awesome link between prayer and mission.

Careful study of the ministry of Jesus as recorded in the gospels and of the early church in the book of Acts, will clearly reveal how prayer became the launch pad for evangelism and mission. In addition to this the power of the Holy Spirit was evidenced both in the ministry of Jesus and subsequently in the ministry of the Apostles. The gospel writers, along with Luke in his account in the Acts, document amazing incidents of changed lives and transformed communities. From the commencement of His ministry, Jesus made it known that He was anointed of the Holy Spirit to "preach the gospel to the poor." For three years He preached this life-changing message combining power with compassion and mercy.

Not only did He preach this message with great power, but He also poured Himself into the lives of the twelve disciples who were with Him. They witnessed at first hand His mighty works and stood in awe and wonder as Jesus not only taught the values of the Kingdom, but also demonstrated its awesome power. These very ordinary men, all from very humble backgrounds, were being prepared for the great task that lay ahead of them, the task of taking this message to the nations of the world. Their mission would be to replicate the ministry of Jesus and to do so with the same level of Holy Spirit anointing. Without this empowering their mission was doomed to failure.

The Mission

> Most assuredly, "I say to you, he who believes in
> Me, the works that I do he will do also; and

175

greater works than these will he do, because I go to My Father."

John 14:12 (N.K.J.V.)

This seems at face value to be an amazing statement made by Jesus given the nature of His mission to date, but He made this statement with an eye to the future. The disciples would indeed follow in the footsteps of their Master in terms of power ministry. They would witness the same miracles of healing, they would see those set free from the power of evil spirits. The greater works would be evidenced in that their ministry would reach to the ends of the earth encompassing all races and cultures. It was exactly this concept of the worldwide church that Jesus had in mind in making this astonishing declaration. Jesus was clearly affirming the role of the Holy Spirit in releasing power to these men in order to accomplish this great task.

John, in this passage, goes on to record the vital role that prayer played as Jesus was in the process of preparing the disciples for what lay ahead,

And I will pray the Father, and He will give you another helper, that He may abide with you forever.

John 14:16 (N.K.J.V.)

"I will pray the Father"

The word "pray" here is translated not in terms of an inferior praying to a superior. Jesus uses this term in the context of praying to His equal. Jesus fully understood that this was an important moment in His relationship with the disciples. He was praying to the Father just hours before going to the cross and He was acutely aware of the weight of responsibility that was about to be placed upon the shoulders of these very ordinary men. It is with great passion that He makes this request to the Father.

"Helper" – Paraclete
(Greek – one called alongside to help)

Jesus, in praying this prayer, was requesting that the disciples, in preparation for this mission, be equipped with the same power and authority that He Himself had demonstrated. The expectation was clear, these men were about to be thrust out into the harvest field to preach the gospel of the Kingdom, and there was the anticipation of a great harvest of souls in response to their ministry. They would face great opposition and persecution, Satan would do all in his power to frustrate them in their task, but this mighty anointing of the Holy Spirit would provide them with the authority not only to stand but to take new ground.

As we look at the church scene today particularly in the West, so much is undertaken through human methodology and ingenuity often leading to frustration and feelings of failure. The man in the street looks on and asks the same question asked by the student at the beginning of this chapter, "What role has the church in 21st century Britain?" There must be, in response to these valid questions, a realisation on the part of the church that only through the enabling power of the Holy Spirit can this message of the gospel be seen to meet the needs of broken people. When people see the life of Jesus manifest in and through the church, they will respond and will desire to know more.

Prayer and the Promise of the Holy Spirit
Luke 24

Luke in this passage is writing about events just following the resurrection of the Lord Jesus Christ. Jesus converses with the two followers on the road to Emmaus. He reminds them of the writings of Moses and the prophets who foretell of His sufferings and subsequent resurrection. The scene then moves back to Jerusalem where we find the disciples gathered amidst reports of Jesus having been seen alive. Then suddenly, the risen Christ appears to them, standing in their midst, and saying to them, "Peace to you." The initial response of the disciples was one of fear, they were convinced they had seen an apparition. Jesus then mildly rebukes them for their doubts and proceeds to remind them, as He did the two on the road to Emmaus, concerning the writings of Moses and the Prophets relative to His sufferings and resurrection. Luke then records the commission given by Jesus to His disciples,

> *And that repentance and remission of sins should be preached in His name to all nations, beginning at Jerusalem. And you are witnesses of these things.*
>
> Luke 24:47-48 (N.K.J.V.)

There then follows a clear instruction for the disciples to remain in Jerusalem to wait upon God for the "promise" of the Holy Spirit,

> *Behold, I send the promise of my father upon you; but tarry in the city of Jerusalem until you are endued with power from on high.*
>
> Luke 24:49 (N.K.J.V.)

Luke also repeats this account in his first chapter of the Acts of the Apostles. Luke begins his Acts' account by making reference to the words spoken by Jesus to the disciples just after His resurrection. They were not to leave Jerusalem, they were to "Wait for the promise of the Father" which would come in a matter of days. The disciples then ask Jesus a question to do with the eventual restoration of the nation of Israel. Jesus responds to their question by pointing out to them that it was not for them to know the times and the seasons that were governed by the sovereign will and purpose of the Father. He did, however, indicate to them that they were about to play a foundational role in the establishing of Kingdom witness beginning at any moment,

> *But you shall receive power when the Holy Spirit has come upon you; and you shall be witnesses to me in Jerusalem, and in all Judea and Samaria, and to the ends of the earth.*
>
> Acts 1:8 (N.K.J.V.)

This was a moment of destiny for the disciples. They had spent three years witnessing at first hand the ministry of Jesus. They had listened to Him as He taught concerning the work and ministry of the Holy Spirit. They had been on an emotional roller-coaster as they witnessed the events surrounding His death and resurrection, and now they were about to be launched on this great mission of preaching the gospel literally to the ends of the then known world. In addition to this, they were about to experience the dynamic of the Holy Spirit in preparation for their task.

The disciples then stood back in awe as they saw Jesus ascend into heaven accompanied by the declaration of the two Angels who stood by them,

> *...This same Jesus, who was taken up from you into heaven, will so come in like manner as you saw Him go into heaven.*
>
> Acts 1:11 (N.K.J.V.)

Following this remarkable train of events, the disciples return to Jerusalem and gather in the upper room. They proceed to spend time in prayer awaiting the outpouring of the Holy Spirit.

Unity

> *These all continued with one accord; (purpose or mind), and supplication, with the women and Mary the mother of Jesus, and with His brothers.*
>
> Acts 1:14 (N.K.J.V.)

The Day of Pentecost
Acts 2

The disciples were being obedient to the instruction given them by Jesus "to tarry in Jerusalem until they be endued with power." The Day of Pentecost arrives and we find them gathered in the upper room praying to the Father. Suddenly, the room is filled with a sound from Heaven like a rushing mighty wind, this sound filled the house where they were sitting.

This was followed by a mighty demonstration of God's power in the form of tongues of fire that rested upon each of them as they prayed. Those gathered were now experiencing this powerful dynamic of the Holy Spirit thus fulfilling the prophecy of Joel some eight hundred years previously,

The Promise of the Holy Spirit

*And it shall come to pass afterward that I will
pour out my Spirit on all flesh; your sons and your
daughters shall prophesy, your old men shall
dream dreams, your young men shall see visions;
and also on My menservants and on My
maidservants I will pour out my Spirit in those
days.*

Joel 2:28-29 (N.K.J.V.)

Peter, in his sermon preached on the Day of Pentecost, made
reference to this prophecy of Joel in response to the accusation
levelled by some in the crowd that the disciples were drunk. Peter
drew their attention to the words of Joel and also reminded them
that the disciples could not be drunk as it was so early in the day.

Not only did this outpouring of the Holy Spirit confirm the
prophecy of Joel, but it also reminded them of Jesus' words in
John 14 when He indicated that He would pray to the Father that
He may send the "helper," the one who would abide with them
for ever. These dramatic events also vindicated the testimony of
John the Baptist when he announced just prior to the baptism of
Jesus,

*I indeed baptise you with water unto repentance,
but he who is coming after me is mightier than I,
whose sandals I am not worthy to carry. He will
baptise you with the Holy Spirit and with fire.*

Matthew 3:11 (N.K.J.V.)

The tongues of fire served as a reminder of the events witnessed
by Moses at the burning bush in Exodus 3. As Moses stood
before the burning bush he noticed that the bush burned with fire
but the bush was not consumed. He was then instructed to remove

his footwear as he was standing on holy ground. Fire symbolises purity and that was to be an essential characteristic in the life of Moses if he was going to accomplish the task God was calling him to. There are several references to fire in scripture often used in connection with the process of purifying, cleansing and empowering. In the same way that Moses was being commissioned at the scene of the burning bush, so the disciples are experiencing the fire of God's awesome presence as they embark upon the mission assigned them by Jesus. This awesome display of holy phenomena accompanied the outpouring of the Holy Spirit upon this company gathered in the upper room. They were all filled with the Spirit and began to speak with other tongues as His power came upon them.

This mighty experience of the baptism of the Holy Spirit was not confined to the four walls of the upper room. It became the dynamic through which the disciples went out onto the streets of Jerusalem and preached the message of the crucified and risen Christ. The city at this particular time was crowded with pilgrims who had journeyed from afar in order to celebrate the Feast of Pentecost. Many of these pilgrims were amazed at what they were seeing and hearing as the disciples, who they knew to be ordinary Galileans, were speaking the languages of their native lands,

> ...*We hear them speaking in our own tongues the wonderful works of God.*
>
> Acts 2:11 (N.K.J.V.)

It is important to note the vital part that prayer played in the events of the Day of Pentecost. They were gathered together in one accord and continued in prayer in response to the instruction given them by Jesus. There was a sense of expectancy among them as they reflected upon the words of Jesus concerning "The

Promise of the Father." There was an awareness among them that something was about to happen that would have dramatic consequences for them and for the testimony of the gospel. Subsequent events were to confirm this anticipation.

The Preaching of Peter

The events of the Day of Pentecost were to bring about a major transformation in the life and ministry of Peter. Just a few weeks prior to this he had vehemently denied even knowing Jesus and issued his denial with oaths and cursing. This particular episode filled Peter with uncontrollable grief as he realised his failure to stand by Jesus in His time of trial. Peter was subsequently restored and was able to come to terms with his failure in response to the grace and compassion shown him by Jesus. This mighty empowerment of the Holy Spirit served to transform Peter from being a belligerent self-opinionated individual, to someone who through this experience became a powerful preacher of the gospel.

Peter confronted the very people instrumental in crucifying Jesus and openly condemned them for their ignorance and wickedness. Their attempt to silence Jesus and put an end to this preaching of the gospel of the Kingdom had totally failed. This same Jesus whom they had crucified in open shame had now been raised from the dead and had destroyed the power of sin and death. The thrust of Peter's preaching was simply the death and resurrection of Jesus and the need for total repentance on their part for their wickedness in perpetrating this terrible deed.

The power of the Holy Spirit began to convict these men of their sin and caused them to be overcome with guilt and shame,

> *Now when they heard this, they were cut to the heart, and said to Peter and the rest of the Apostles, "Men and brethren, what shall we do?"*
>
> Acts 2:37 (N.K.J.V.)

Peter's Response

> *...Repent, and let every one of you be baptised in the name of Jesus Christ for the remission of sins; and you shall receive the gift of the Holy Spirit.*
>
> Acts 2:38 (N.K.J.V.)

This promise of the Holy Spirit was not just the special privilege of the disciples; it was a promise open to all including those who were afar off, as many as the Lord would call (Joel 2).

Not only did Peter's preaching expose the cruelty of the Jewish religious leaders, but it also touched the hearts of the people thronging the city streets.

A Mighty Harvest

The message of the gospel was preached with such power that by the end of the day, 3,000 people had been added to their number. Following this harvest a powerful church was established, and an immediate impact was made upon the community.

Church Order
The Ministry of Prayer

> *And they continued steadfastly in the Apostles' doctrine and fellowship, in the breaking of bread, and in prayer.*
>
> *Acts 2:42 (N.K.J.V.)*

Prayer was foundational to the life and witness of the early church. From the Day of Pentecost onwards, prayer became the power through which the life and testimony of the church was conducted. The word "steadfast" implies a devotion to the discipline of prayer borne of a realisation that failure to engage will only result in weakness and loss. This level of prayer served to promote a fear of God and an appreciation of the awesomeness of His presence,

> *Then fear came upon every soul, and many wonders and signs were done through the apostles.*
>
> Acts 2:43 (N.K.J.V.)

A sense of reverential awe permeated the fellowship as the power of the Holy Spirit began to be manifest in their midst. The signs and wonders promised by Jesus became a prominent feature in the life of these early believers. The Apostles, supported by the prayers of the people, were enabled to replicate the ministry of Jesus, and witnessed the transforming power of the gospel on a daily basis. The message of the Kingdom of God was preached with great power and authority.

In addition to their devotion to fellowship, teaching, breaking of bread and prayer, there was a determination on the part of all to address the needs of the poor.

The early church met in houses and were therefore not committed to the upkeep of buildings and other such overheads. Those among them who had disposable income saw to it that every material need was met and that no one was disadvantaged due to lack of financial resources. Initially they remained as part of the temple community, but their house gatherings became the springboard for mission and outreach.

Evangelism was at the heart of their activity as they sought to be obedient to the mandate given them by Jesus. There was a resolve to model their ministry on the ministry of Jesus and this was clearly seen in their commitment to evangelism, prayer, power, compassion and help to the poor. Every believer was encouraged to be part of this vision.

Conclusion
The Promise of the Holy Spirit

Reference has already been made to the anointing of the Holy Spirit that rested upon Jesus as He went about His earthly ministry. We have seen how He spent three years mentoring and training His disciples for the task of mission. He taught them concerning the life and power of the Holy Spirit in relation to ministry. To attempt such an undertaking through the means of human methodology would simply be doomed to failure. We have seen that this whole process began with a prayer uttered by Jesus,

> *And I will pray the father, and He will give you another helper that He may abide with you forever.*
>
> John 14:16 (N.K.J.V.)

The implementation of the "Great Commission," and the task of world mission began with this prayer of Jesus. It was answered on the Day of Pentecost as the disciples were endued with the power of the Holy Spirit. There was a clear understanding right from the early stages of the life of this new community that the power of the Holy Spirit was given principally for mission. Major challenges would have to be faced by these early believers not least the threat of persecution. To claim to be a follower of Jesus would cost many of them their lives or at least lengthy prison sentences.

Within a generation the message of the gospel had been proclaimed throughout the then known world resulting in the birthing of vibrant communities of witness that would impact the major cities of the Roman Empire.

Prayer and the Holy Spirit

Jesus had been teaching the principle of asking, seeking and knocking,

> *If you then, being evil, know how to give good gifts to your children, how much more will your Heavenly Father give the Holy Spirit to those who ask Him?*
>
> Luke 11:13 (N.K.J.V.)

The church in our day needs to engage in prayer at this level as she seeks to respond to the great challenge of the hour. There are forces determined to silence the testimony of the gospel and in so doing unleash a tide of lawlessness in our society. The church must awake out of her slumber and come before the face of God in prayer for the sake of the nation.

When believers rise to this challenge and engage on this level the question of the young student referred to at the beginning of this chapter will be answered with sincerity and integrity; yes – the church does have a vital role to play in 21st century Britain.

Jesus

> *...If anyone thirsts, let him come to Me and drink.*
> *He who believes in Me, as the scripture has said,*
> *out of his heart will flow rivers of living water.*
>
> John 7:37-38 (N.K.J.V.)

Are you thirsty?

Chapter 10

Strategy For Mission

Having examined the vital role that prayer played in the outpouring of the Holy Spirit upon the disciples on the Day of Pentecost, we now take this a stage further by discovering the power of prayer in relation to evangelism and mission. The events recorded by Luke in the book of Acts serve to remind us of the principles of ministry established by Jesus during His time here on earth. The heart of Jesus was for the lost and His purpose was to expose and then destroy the works of Satan, particularly with reference to sin and sickness. Mention has already been made how Jesus, in exercising His powerful ministry, not only sought to meet the needs of the people, but also mentored His disciples in preparation for the task of preaching the gospel of the Kingdom in the power of the Holy Spirit.

Following the Day of Pentecost, it is clear to see that the motivation of these early disciples was mission. There was a determination on their part that this visitation and manifestation of the Spirit's power should not be confined to the four walls of their meeting place. This is a danger that the church needs to guard against during this season in which the Spirit is being

189

poured out in renewing power. The words spoken by Jesus were still at the forefront of their minds when He indicated to them that the Spirit's power would enable them to be "Witnesses." This declaration of the gospel of the Kingdom would be attested by the presence of awesome signs and wonders as the disciples replicated the ministry of Jesus. As we read through Luke's account of the mission of the early church, we see this great thrust of evangelism commencing on the streets of Jerusalem and then fanning out to Judea, Samaria, and eventually spreading to the great cities of the Roman Empire. Communities of believers were established in these strategic centres of commerce as multitudes responded to the message of the cross and resurrection of Jesus Christ.

The purpose of this chapter is to examine some of the incidents in which prayer is clearly seen to be the strategy behind effective mission. We shall see how prayer and mission are inextricably linked and that to attempt to launch out on any evangelistic programme without saturating it in prayer is at best a futile exercise.

The Healing of the Lame Man
Acts 3

Peter and John were walking toward the temple at the "hour of prayer." In the previous chapter it was noted that the new community of believers met in houses, but they continued to be faithful to the activities of the temple.

As Peter and John were approaching, they encountered a lame man who had been in that condition since birth. Every day, for years, he had been placed at the "Beautiful" gate of the temple, and there he would beg as worshippers entered to conduct their act of worship. This was nothing less than a situation of human misery as day after day he sat there in the hope that some may just take pity on him.

When he saw Peter and John approaching, he cried out to gain the attention of the two disciples. Little did this poor man know that he was about to be centre stage in a series of events that would not only dramatically change his life, but would also have a major impact in the temple courts and precincts.

As Peter and John looked upon this pitiful sight, there was the immediate realisation that "silver and gold" could not help him. Only the mighty healing power of Jesus, manifested in His Name, could meet this lame man at his point of need,

> *Then Peter said, "Silver and gold I do not have, but what I do have I give to you: in the name of Jesus Christ of Nazareth, rise up and walk." And he took him by the right hand and lifted him up, and immediately his feet and ankle bones received strength.*
>
> Acts 3:6-7 (N.K.J.V.)

There followed scenes of unprecedented joy as the lame man, in response to the words of Peter, immediately stood up and entered the temple leaping and praising God. The onlookers stood by marvelling at the unfolding of these dramatic events. The lame man, who had been placed at this same spot every day for years, was now the centre of attention as he walked and leapt in the temple precincts. This miracle provided Peter and John with the opportunity to preach the gospel to the crowds who by now were flocking to the scene. They gave clear emphasis to the message of the Cross of Christ and His resurrection making reference to the many scriptures that foretold these events. Peter and John drew their attention to the writings of Moses and the prophets, all of whom gave clear indicators concerning Jesus and the nature of His ministry. There was a clear call for repentance and a turning away from sin so that "times of refreshing" may come from the presence of the Lord.

Acts 4
Peter and John arrested

Following these dramatic events, the Priests and the Sadducees took great exception to the scenes of excitement that were evident around the temple precincts. They were particularly disturbed at the preaching of the resurrection from the dead, they therefore issued immediate orders for the arrest of Peter and John. Their arrest did nothing to dampen the ardour of the gathered company of people. Many came to faith in Christ and their number increased to about five thousand.

Peter and John were summoned to appear before the religious rulers and were asked by what power or in whose name was this miracle performed? Far from being constrained by their court appearance, Peter and John used the opportunity to once again boldly declare the message of Jesus Christ, His death and resurrection. It was through the name of Jesus, and by no other power, that this lame man stood before them whole. When the council saw the boldness of the two disciples and realised that they were uneducated men, they marvelled and concluded that these two men had been in the presence of Jesus. The sight of the lame man standing before them fully restored, the reaction of the people, and the boldness of the two disciples added great power and credibility to the witness of the gospel. The religious rulers realised that they had boxed themselves into a corner and were in danger of heaping ridicule upon themselves. In order to find some fig leaf of credibility, they warned Peter and John to never again preach in the name of Jesus. Failure to comply with this order would have serious consequences for the men possibly resulting in their deaths.

Boldness

> ...*Whether it is right in the sight of God to listen to you more than to God, you judge. For we cannot but speak the things which we have seen and heard.*
>
> Acts 4:19-20 (N.K.J.V.)

Such was the level of Holy Spirit anointing upon them, Peter and John would allow nothing to stand in the way of the preaching of the gospel. The threats of the religious rulers were rendered ineffective by the boldness demonstrated by the Apostles.

Having been warned to never again preach in the name of Jesus, Peter and John return to their companions and report to them the sequence of events surrounding their "trial." There follows one of the most powerful prayer meetings recorded in the whole of scripture, the climax of which would witness a powerful manifestation of the Holy Spirit which would literally cause the building in which they were meeting to shake!

This threat, delivered by the religious council, served to galvanise the believers and to draw them together in prayer. They *"Lifted their voice to God with one accord."* This signifies a unity of purpose in their praying and must surely provide for us today a powerful "model" when engaging in prayer at this level. Their unity provided a solid platform from which strategic prayer could be launched. Reference is made to the words of the Psalmist recorded in Psalm 2 when he speaks of the "raging of nations" and the determination of kings and rulers to stand against the Lord and against His anointed, saying,

> *Let us break their bonds asunder, and cast away their cords from us.*
>
> Psalm 2:3 (N.K.J.V.)

The opposition now being experienced by the disciples stood as confirmation of the words of the Psalmist,

> *Now, Lord, look on their threats, and grant to your servants that with all boldness they may speak Your word, by stretching out your hand to heal, and that signs and wonders may be done through the name of your Holy Servant Jesus.*
>
> Acts 4:29-30 (N.K.J.V.)

This was not a prayer requesting protection from any threat that may come their way. It was not a prayer based upon some attempt to "accommodate" the demands of the council. This was a prayer asking for an even greater degree of boldness, enabling them to preach the gospel in the name of Jesus, not only in their own locality, but in the regions beyond. In addition to this, their prayer contained a request asking God to confirm the preaching of the gospel with mighty signs and wonders and miracles of healing.

The Aftermath of this Prayer

> *And when they had prayed, the place where they were assembled together was shaken; and they*

> *were all filled with the Holy Spirit, and they spoke*
> *the word of God with boldness.*
>
> Acts 4:31(N.K.J.V.)

This powerful dimension of prayer not only gave the believers a spirit of boldness, but it also drew them together to the extent that they were "of one heart and one soul." They witnessed rapid growth as the preaching of the gospel continued unabated. Miracles and signs and wonders were in evidence, and there was a determination amongst them to address the needs of the poor.

Power

> *And with great power the Apostles gave witness to*
> *the resurrection of the Lord Jesus. And great*
> *grace was upon them all.*
>
> Acts 4:33 (N.K.J.V.)

The story of the early church continues as described by Luke in his account recorded in the book of Acts. The gospel continued to be preached with great power, and multitudes were added to their number. Powerful miracles of healing were in evidence as sick folk were literally brought out into the streets of the city. Luke describes that people would even sit under the shadow of Peter expecting to receive healing. This powerful move of the Holy Spirit brought in its wake a tide of persecution and the Apostles found themselves in prison on account of their witness and testimony. They receive an angelic visitation in the prison resulting in an amazing release, much to the consternation of the high priest and elders of Israel who had arrested them. Standing before the bemused authorities who had authorised their arrest, Peter once again takes the opportunity to declare the message of

Jesus Christ and His death and resurrection. Such was the fury of the religious leaders, they began to take measures to kill the Apostles. Their lives were saved through the timely intervention of Gamaliel, a respected teacher of the Law, who urged caution upon his colleagues in respect to their treatment of these men.

The life and witness of the church continued with the number of disciples multiplying both among the Hebrews and the Greek speaking Jews. A situation arose, recorded by Luke in the sixth chapter of Acts, that had the potential to bring serious division and unrest. It warranted the immediate attention of the Apostles so as to avert any serious damage to their testimony.

In dealing with this potentially difficult issue, the Apostles re-affirmed the priority of prayer and the ministry of the word of God.

Church Dispute
Acts 6

Foundational to the practice of the early church was care for the poor and in particular the widows. Widows were often left destitute if they had no family and were prey for all manner of unscrupulous money lenders. Careful attention was given to this matter and it had always been the practice for widows to be looked after. The dispute arose between two sets of widows, there were the Hebrew widows, and the Greek speaking (Hellenists) widows. The Greeks felt that they were being disadvantaged in the disposal of the funds in that they were receiving less than their Hebrew counterparts. This became a contentious issue resulting in a sharp disagreement that threatened to disrupt their unity and purpose. The Apostles, seeing the potential danger, sought to deal with the matter head on, and in doing so established clear guidelines as to how such matters should be resolved in the life of the church.

They instructed the people to seek out seven men of good reputation, full of the Holy Spirit and wisdom to administer the funds. The appointment of these seven men would free the Apostles from having to be involved in matters that were purely administrative. It would enable them to concentrate on the ministry that God had called them to. This must not be misconstrued as the Apostles minimising the importance of such matters, they were of the utmost importance and required the expertise of godly men who were full of the Holy Spirit, and blessed with the gift of "administration." One of their number was Stephen, *"A man full of faith and the Holy Spirit."*

> *But we will give ourselves continually to prayer and to the ministry of the word.*
>
> *Acts 6:4 (N.K.J.V.)*

The Apostles quickly recognised the ploy of the enemy in seeking to sow seeds of discord within the fellowship, thus creating a situation in which administrative matters would take up their valuable time.

Prayer Strategy

> *Whom they set before the Apostles; and when they had prayed, they laid hands on them.*
>
> Acts 6:6 (N.K.J.V.)

Mission Strategy

> *Then the word of the Lord spread, and the number of disciples multiplied greatly in Jerusalem, and a*

> *great many of the priests were obedient to the faith.*
>
> Acts 6:7 (N.K.J.V.)

Stephen, full of faith and power, did great wonders and signs among the people. This potentially divisive matter was settled in a spirit of wisdom, and served to release seven men into powerful ministry roles, and reinforced the position of the Apostles thus enabling them to focus their priorities on prayer and the ministry of the word of God.

There are important lessons to learn from this incident for church life today. There are too many leaders involved in matters for which they are not called. There is an urgent need for leaders to concentrate on their priority calling, namely, prayer and preaching!

Growth and Persecution

The remarkable story of the life and witness of these early believers continues to unfold as we read further into the book of Acts. Stephen, this mighty man, full of faith and power, was mightily used in the preaching of the gospel and in the working of signs and wonders. It was not long before a tide of persecution hit this company of believers, and Stephen found himself at the receiving end of false accusations. In chapter seven we have the full transcript of his defence made before the council. His defence takes the form of a potted history of God's dealings with the nation of Israel. Stephen openly accuses them of their blindness in failing to recognise Jesus for who He was. He spoke with such power and authority that his accusers were struck down with fury as his message hit home and exposed their hypocrisy. Such was their fury they rushed upon Stephen in a fit of rage and he fell under a hail of stones.

As the stones were being hurled at Stephen, he, in his dying moments saw the heavens opened and the Son of Man standing at the right hand of God. Stephen became the first martyr of the Christian church and the manner of his death was a portent for things to come. Standing in the midst of those who were throwing stones was a young Jewish zealot by the name of Saul of Tarsus. His duty that day was to look after the coats of the stone throwers, but there was residing in his spirit an abiding hatred of the church and a determination to play a lead role in silencing her witness.

Following the death of Stephen this tide of persecution intensified with many of the believers being "scattered abroad" who went everywhere preaching the word. Their number included Philip who went down to the city of Samaria and preached Christ. Multitudes came to faith in Christ and mighty miracles of healing were very much in evidence.

The Conversion of Saul

Saul, this ardent Pharisee, was on a one man mission to eradicate the church. As he was travelling on the road to Damascus, he encountered the Lord Jesus Christ. Saul was immediately overcome by the brightness of the light that shone around him, causing him to fall off his horse. Saul's conversion was to be a turning point in the history of the early church in that the one who had up until this point been her most vociferous enemy, had now become her most powerful convert. In spite of this tide of persecution, the witness and testimony of the church grew,

Then the churches throughout all Judea, Galilee, and Samaria had peace and were edified. And walking in the fear of the Lord and in the comfort of the Holy Spirit, they were multiplied.

Acts 9:31 (N.K.J.V.)

Following the conversion of Saul, (who later became Paul), Peter embarked upon a mission that took him to various parts including Lydda. A notable miracle took place at Lydda through the ministry of Peter involving a man by the name of Aenas who had been bedridden for eight years. Peter, ministering under a powerful anointing of the Holy Spirit, proclaims healing for Aenas causing him to immediately arise and take his bed away with him. Luke goes on to record how all who lived in Lydda and Sharon saw Aenas and subsequently turned to the Lord.

Acts 9

A small distance from Lydda, where Peter had been ministering, was the town of Joppa. There was a small company of believers at Joppa, one of their number being a very dearly loved lady by the name of Dorcas. She was full of good deeds and was involved in the pursuit of charitable acts. Suddenly, she was taken ill and died, much to the distress of her fellow believers. When those in Joppa heard that Peter was ministering in nearby Lydda, they sent two of their number imploring him to come to Joppa.

He arrived and was confronted with a scene of great sorrow as the believers mourned Dorcas' death.

The Power of Prayer

> *But Peter put them all out, and knelt down and*
> *prayed. And turning to the body he said, "Tabitha,*
> *arise." And she opened her eyes, and when she*
> *saw Peter she sat up.*
>
> Acts 9:40 (N.K.J.V.)

There was great rejoicing, as the company of believers received Dorcas back to life. This miracle, wrought through the passionate prayer of Peter, had major implications for the growth of the church in that community,

> *And it became known throughout all Joppa, and*
> *many believed on the Lord.*
>
> Acts 9:24 (N.K.J.V.)

This incident in the life of Peter powerfully illustrates the link that exists between prayer and powerful mission strategy. It is clear from reading the book of Acts that where mission is undertaken in response to prevailing prayer, the potential exists for multitudes to come to faith in Christ.

Cornelius
Acts 10

Following the events in Joppa, Peter spends a period of time in the house of Simon. The beginning of chapter 10 marks a significant event in the life and witness of the early church and in particular for Peter as he continues his ministry. To date the church was composed of Jews who had come to faith in Christ and had received the gift of the Holy Spirit. There remained that residual hostility even in the hearts of these early believers toward the Gentiles, and any thought of this gospel being received by Gentiles was still an anathema to many of the Jewish believers. This was about to change through a process of events culminating in the salvation of Cornelius and his household, all of whom were Gentiles. This incident heralded the commencement of gospel witness to the gentiles thus establishing the church of Jesus Christ as a body that embraced all races and cultures. In addition to this, prayer was to play a key role in the development of the story,

> *A devout man and one who feared God with all his household, who gave alms generously to the people, and prayed to God always.*
>
> Acts 10:2 (N.K.J.V.)

Cornelius was a Roman military officer who was in command of one hundred men. In order for him to attain to this rank, he would have needed to be a hard, and in many ways a ruthless man – a man who commanded immediate respect from all who came into contact with him. This military bearing, however, appeared to be just one side of his personality. Luke records how Cornelius showed piety and was devoted to helping the poor. He was also a man who clearly understood the importance of prayer in that he was willing to spend time before God on behalf of others. It was while Cornelius was in prayer, about the ninth hour of the day, 3pm, that he witnessed a train of events that would have major consequences for him and his family, but also for Peter and all believers. As he was praying he saw a vision in which he saw an angel of God coming and saying to him, "Cornelius." His immediate reaction was one of fear as he enquired as to the reason behind this angelic visitation.

The Angelic Instruction

> *"What is it Lord" So He said to him, "your*
> *prayers and your alms have come up before God*
> *as a memorial. Now send men to Joppa, and send*
> *for Simon whose surname is Peter."*
>
> Acts 10:4-5 (N.K.J.V.)

Cornelius immediately sends two of his men to seek out Peter in Joppa. One of the most compelling aspects of this story is the way in which prayer was at the centre of the circumstances of both Peter and the centurion. We have seen how Cornelius was in prayer when he received the angelic visitation. Whilst all of this was happening to Cornelius, and as his two messengers were travelling toward Joppa, Peter was engaged in prayer as he sat on the rooftop of his house awaiting a meal,

> *...Peter went to the housetop to pray, about the*
> *sixth hour.*
>
> Acts 10:9 (N.K.J.V.)

As Peter was praying, he was suddenly in the midst of a trance in which he saw an object like a great white sheet bound at the four corners, descending to him on the rooftop. In the trance Peter observed all kinds of four footed animals, wild beasts, creeping things, and birds of the air. Peter was then instructed to "arise and eat." This command flew in the face of Peter's Jewish pedigree in that all such creatures were rendered unclean according to Jewish ceremonial law. The Lord then spoke to Peter words that would have a profound effect upon him, Cornelius and his household, and the whole future mission strategy of the early church,

... Rise, Peter, kill and eat.

Acts 10:13 (N.K.J.V.)

Peter refused on the grounds that the contents of the sheet were unclean and were not to be regarded by a Jew.

A Second Invitation

> *And a voice came to him again a second time, "what God has cleansed you must not call common."*
>
> Acts 10:15 (N.K.J.V.)

This exercise was repeated three times before the sheet was taken up into heaven again. Naturally speaking, Peter was greatly disturbed by this vision and its implications. While he was pondering these events, the two messengers sent by Cornelius arrived at the house he was staying seeking his whereabouts. Peter was instructed to greet the two men and to have an open mind concerning the reason behind their call; they had been sent by God and it was important for Peter to understand this.

Peter and the two men, along with a number of believers from Joppa, journey toward the house of Cornelius in Caesarea. They find Cornelius waiting for them along with a retinue of family and friends. Following the exchange of greetings, Peter and Cornelius begin their conversation.

Peter commenced his statement by reminding the gathered company how it was unlawful for a Jewish man to associate or to even be in the presence of one from another nation. This cultural and religious paradigm shift in the thinking of Peter was to be foundational in the opening up of the gospel message to the gentiles. Having made reference to his initial hesitancy in accepting the invitation to visit Cornelius, Peter shares how God had clearly shown him that it was wrong to call any man common or unclean.

The story then unfolds, as Cornelius recounts the events surrounding the angelic visitation he had received and of the command given to send men to Joppa to summon Peter. The stage was now set for Peter to preach to the gathered company made up of Jew and Gentile. This was one of the most momentous events in the history of the early church. Peter boldly declares that God is no respecter of persons, and that all men are equal in His sight. Peter proceeds to preach the message of Jesus Christ beginning with the baptism of John, up to and including His mighty works of power demonstrated during His earthly ministry. Peter then brings his message to a climax as he focuses attention on the cross, the sufferings of Christ and of His subsequent resurrection. Cornelius and his circle of friends were left in no doubt that this gift of salvation, made possible by Christ's work on the cross, is open to all who believe in Him. There is also the assurance of sins forgiven.

A New Dimension of Mission

> *While Peter was still speaking these words, the Holy Spirit fell upon all who heard the word.*
>
> Acts 10:44 (N.K.J.V.)

This was to herald a dramatic breakthrough in the life of the early church. Gentiles were now receiving the message of the gospel and were coming to faith in Christ. Not only that, but they were also experiencing the mighty infilling of the Holy Spirit as they glorified God and spoke in other tongues. The Jewish believers who had come with Peter were amazed at what they were seeing. Following their conversion and their receiving of the Holy Spirit, they were baptised in the name of the Lord Jesus Christ. The events that took place that day in the house of Cornelius paved the way for the gospel to be preached to "all nations." The glory of the church was to be shown in the uniting of Jew and Gentile under the Lordship of Jesus Christ.

These glorious events were bound together in that Cornelius the Gentile and Peter the Jew were both in prayer before God. Prayer became the catalyst in bringing these two men together. They were culturally and racially apart, but became one in Christ Jesus. The way was open for the gospel to be preached to the nations of Europe and for vibrant communities of believers to be established in the major cities of the Roman Empire.

One of the great strengths of the church today is that she has in her ranks believers from every race and culture, each expressing their love for Jesus consistent with their language and traditions. From all of these people groups, God is building a mighty prayer army that is instrumental in bringing many to faith in Christ.

The Antioch Church
Acts 13

We are going to examine one more incident recorded in the Acts of the Apostles in which prayer became the launch pad and catalyst for mission. Following the tide of persecution directed against the church in Jerusalem, we read that believers were scattered, but wherever they went they preached Christ. It is often said that persecution can sometimes act as a fire that ignites the hearts of believers drawing them closer to God and to each other, and renewing zeal in matters relative to prayer and mission. After the death of Stephen, groups of believers were dispersed to Cyprus and Phoenicia, but some went as far as Antioch. They came with a passion to preach the gospel and to see the Kingdom of God demonstrated through mighty signs and wonders. Luke records how a great number turned to the Lord as His hand of blessing rested upon their endeavours.

When the Apostles at Jerusalem heard that the gospel had been preached in Antioch, they sent Barnabas on a fact-finding mission. He was asked to observe this young group of believers and then report back to the leaders at Jerusalem his findings. Barnabas was able to give a positive report confirming that the work at Antioch was a genuine move of the Holy Spirit, and that the fellowship was blessed with strong leadership. He encouraged them to continue in the faith and to serve the Lord with purpose of heart.

A Healthy Church

There was a strong foundation supporting the work in Antioch in that right from its early days there was a commitment to godly leadership and a zeal to win souls for Jesus. There was also a dedication to prayer and intercession, and it is quite clear from this narrative that prayer played a vital role particularly in support of mission strategy. A strong leadership team made up of prophets and teachers provided the assembly with balance. Every major decision was arrived at following seasons of waiting upon God, and very often supported by systematic fasting. Their abiding passion was that at all times, their outreach and ministry should be directed by the Holy Spirit,

> *As they ministered to the Lord and fasted, the Holy*
> *Spirit said, "Now separate to me Barnabas and*
> *Saul for the work to which I have called them."*
> *Then having fasted and prayed, and laid hands on*
> *them, they sent them away.*
>
> Acts 13:2-3 (N.K.J.V.)

The Holy Spirit and Prayer

It is worthy of note here that there were factors in operation that were conducive to the manifestation of the Holy Spirit's power. The believers were clearly in unity as they sought the Lord. Their hearts were in tune with the will of God in that the focus of their prayer was mission and the salvation of the lost. The leadership was made up of men who were not exercising their roles purely upon the basis of status, but they were men who had a heart for God, and for reaching out. In addition their sincerity was clearly demonstrated in their readiness to fast as they sought the mind of God. This pattern of church life recorded here in chapter 13 ought to provide the "model" for church life today, and in particular the way in which evangelism and mission is approached.

We must also observe that this sending of Barnabas and Saul was not the work of the church, this was God giving clear direction in response to their seasons of prayer and fasting. They went from Antioch preaching the gospel in the synagogues.

Following their commissioning by the Antioch church, Paul, as he became known, and Barnabas embarked upon a missionary journey preaching the gospel of the Kingdom, and seeing mighty signs and wonders and miracles of healing. Chapters 13 and 14 of Acts document the amazing scenes as the two evangelists preach to great crowds of people. Luke records how through their preaching, the Word of God was spread throughout all the region. It was not long before the activities of Paul and Barnabas attracted the attention of those who sought to oppose their message resulting in their expulsion from that particular city. Their mission extended to the region of Iconium where they spoke boldly in the name of the Lord Jesus resulting in the salvation of many and as in previous ministry situations, the manifestation of signs and wonders. From there they journeyed to the cities of Derbe and Lystra, and it was at Lystra where Paul witnessed one of the most remarkable miracles of healing in his entire ministry.

Luke records how that at Lystra, there was a man who had been a cripple from birth,

> *This man heard Paul speaking. Paul, observing him intently and seeing that he had faith to be healed, said with a loud voice, stand up straight on your feet! And he leaped and walked.*
>
> Acts 14:9-10 (N.K.J.V.)

This was by no means an isolated incident in the experience of the two evangelists as they faithfully sought to preach the gospel in the power of the Holy Spirit.

Conclusion

These mighty acts of Paul and Barnabas were birthed through the seasons of prayer and fasting undertaken by the Antioch church. There is a clear strategy for mission recorded here by Luke as he relates the story of the ministry and mission of the believers in Antioch. A passion to win people for Jesus was backed up by prayer and fasting and the casting of vision by godly leaders who operated only through the prompting of the Holy Spirit and not by any human agenda.

There are clear lessons to learn from this story for the church today as she seeks to communicate this great message of the gospel to a "post-modern" and in some cases a "post Christian" society. Effective mission can only be conducted through prayer and a total reliance upon the power and dynamic of the Holy Spirit.

As they ministered to the Lord and fasted, the Holy Spirit said...

Chapter 11

Prayer and the Growth
of the Believer

From the moment a person comes to faith in Christ, a process of growth begins and continues up until the day he or she dies. Just as in the natural a newborn baby immediately begins to grow, so the believer matures as the life of Christ becomes more evident in their daily lives. The Apostle Paul gives very clear teaching in relation to the spiritual growth of the Christian,

> *Being confident of this very thing, that He who has begun a good work in you will complete it until the day of Jesus Christ.*
>
> Philippians 1:6 (N.K.J.V.)

Spiritual growth is a subject that burned within the heart of the great apostle. He urges believers to continue in the faith and not to be distracted with issues of lesser importance. Paul, in taking up this theme, is confirming the teaching of Jesus concerning the importance of "abiding in the vine."

211

*If you abide in Me, and My words abide in you,
you will ask what you desire, and it will be done
for you. By this My Father is glorified, that you
bear much fruit; so you will be my disciples.*

John 15:7-8 (N.K.J.V.)

Jesus goes on to speak in terms of the believer being appointed to go and bear fruit, and that the fruit should remain. This same burden is clearly seen in the heart of Paul as he prays for all believers. He prays that they may at all times walk worthy of their calling, that they may increase in their knowledge of God, and that they may be fruitful in every good work.

The purpose of this chapter is to examine the two prayers prayed by Paul recorded in his epistle to the Ephesians. Both of these prayers are to do with the spiritual growth of the believer, and both give clear indication of the great concern that Paul had for the church of Jesus Christ.

Paul and Prayer

So much could be written and spoken concerning the life and ministry of this remarkable servant of God. His courage in the face of persecution and opposition, coupled with his zeal to win the lost are but two of the trade marks of Paul's life and service. Prayer became the foundation upon which his entire ministry was built. He not only prayed for the success of his mission and for the opening of greater doors of opportunity, but he also prayed with great passion for individual believers to be effective in reaching out to others with the good news of the gospel. He begins several of his epistles assuring his readers that he was remembering them in his prayers night and day.

It is worth remembering that he was often writing from a prison cell, cut off from the warmth of Christian fellowship, and yet it is very evident in his writings that he was with them in spirit. His immense care and concern for the churches is powerfully demonstrated in the form of these two prayers written in the Ephesian epistle.

Ephesus

The city of Ephesus became one of the most strategic centres for gospel witness in the early church. It was a major centre of commerce and trade and was a major seaport that served the great trade routes of the Mediterranean. It shared with Syrian Antioch and Egyptian Alexandria the honour of being one of the three great cities of the Eastern part of the Roman Empire. In addition to its commercial importance, Ephesus was very much a cosmopolitan city with a population being drawn from several nations including a large Jewish community. Ephesus was also a major religious centre, its life being dominated by the great temple erected to the worship of the goddess Diana. This great temple was one of the Seven Wonders of the ancient world and became the principal landmark of Ephesus. Worship of the goddess Diana involved the practice of grotesque occultic acts, this was accompanied by the presence of legalised prostitution. It was against this background that a thriving centre of gospel witness was established which impacted not only the religious life of the city, but also its commercial life. These events are recorded by Luke in the eighteenth and nineteenth chapters of the book of Acts.

The epistle to the Ephesians, along with Colossians, Philippians and Philemon, was written by Paul whilst he was in prison in

Rome. He commences the letter by reminding the believers that he was an apostle of Jesus Christ by the will of God and not through the appointment of men. He addresses the letter to the *"Saints who are in Ephesus, and to the faithful in Christ Jesus."* Many commentators regard the Ephesian epistle as the "Magnum Opus", or the "masterpiece" of Paul's letters. In it he teaches concerning the riches of God's grace and the position of the believer in Christ Jesus. The first of these two great prayers prayed by Paul is recorded in the first chapter. It follows on from a passage in which he sets out the spiritual blessings that are the possession of every disciple of Jesus Christ.

The Source of these Blessings

> *Blessed be the God and Father of our Lord Jesus Christ, who has blessed us with every spiritual blessing in the heavenly places in Christ.*
>
> Ephesians 1:3 (N.K.J.V.)

In writing these words, Paul is seeking to set out the great objective of this letter, namely, that all believers may grasp and hold on to a firm understanding of the greatness and glory of Father God. Paul refers to Him as *"The God and Father of our Lord Jesus Christ"*, *"The Father of Glory."* Paul is anxious for his readers to fully understand this truth concerning the greatness and majesty of God.

From verses four to fourteen, Paul lists in detail the nature of these "spiritual blessings." We could devote pages looking into each of these great blessings, but that is not the purpose of this book. We can however list them in order:

Spiritual blessings – blessed – chosen – predestined – adopted – accepted – redeemed – forgiven – enlightened – given an inheritance – sealed – assured.

All of these are conferred upon every believer from the moment they come to faith in Jesus Christ. Paul, as he meditates upon these incredible blessings, is overcome with a great sense of joy, and he finds himself giving thanks to God for the love that he has lavished upon each one of His children. Something of the heart of Paul, both in his love for God, and his love for the church is clearly seen in this prayer.

The Growth of the Believer

Thanksgiving

> *Therefore I also, after I heard of your faith in the Lord Jesus and your love for all the saints, do not cease to give thanks for you, making mention of you in my prayers.*
>
> Ephesians 1:15-16 (N.K.J.V.)

"Therefore"

This is a key word in Paul's prayer in that it acts as a link between the preceding passage we have just referred to and to the teaching on "spiritual blessings" in particular. Paul continues to be overwhelmed at the scope of this glorious revelation and the implications they present to every individual believer. The prayer that follows is a response from the heart of the apostle, and it is an earnest cry for these great truths to be fully understood by all who profess to be followers of Jesus Christ.

Paul's Motive for Praying

Quite apart from his own sense of awe at the unfolding revelation of these "spiritual blessings", he realises that it is of paramount importance that a firm grasp of this truth be held by all believers. There must also be a clear understanding that all of this comes from the heart of God and has nothing to do with status or position. Paul, in writing to the Ephesians, is rejoicing at their salvation. He is greatly encouraged as he hears about their faith in the Lord Jesus, and of their love for the saints. This joy, welling up within the heart of the apostle inspires him to pen this majestic prayer calling for there to be a continuation in their growth and maturity.

A Spirit of Revelation

> That the God of our Lord Jesus Christ, the Father
> of Glory, may give you the Spirit of wisdom and
> revelation in the knowledge of Him.
>
> Ephesians 1:17 (N.K.J.V.)

Right from the commencement of this prayer, it is clear to see that Paul's burden is for the growth and maturing of their faith. Whenever Paul encountered believers who had lost their vision, or who had become static in their walk with God, his heart was always saddened. For Paul, such a situation was a contradiction in terms. The Christian life by nature is a life of growth and development, and so for Paul there had to be that evidence of spiritual growth. This is a principle that needs to be taken on board in our lives as believers today. So often the life and testimony of the Christian community is hamstrung by a failure to grow and to move on with God. So often in our pastoral ministry we are dealing with issues that just seem to manifest themselves on a continual basis with very few signs of growth and victory. God's purpose for each and every one of His children is for growth and to bear fruit.

With this uppermost in his mind, Paul prays directly to *"The God of our Lord Jesus Christ, the Father of Glory"*, the one who has conferred on them these incredible "spiritual blessings'. He asks that God may give them, *"The Spirit of wisdom and revelation in the knowledge of Him."* I particularly like the N.I.V. rendering of this verse,

> *I keep asking that the God of our Lord Jesus Christ, the Glorious Father, may give you the spirit of wisdom and revelation, so that you may know Him better.*
>
> Ephesians 1:17 (N.I.V.)

This translation really expresses the heart of Paul as he prays for the saints in Ephesus. He is asking that they may experience a dimension of Holy Spirit power enabling them to see a clearer picture of the working of God's word in their hearts and lives. He also asks that there may be this increasing measure of the glory of Jesus Christ, and a more mature understanding of His will and purpose for them. The revelation that Paul prays about here has to do with the imparting of knowledge, and it comes as the believer cultivates the discipline of systematic and diligent study. Hunger for truth will cause the heart to be open to receive and take on board the revelation that God desires to impart.

If "revelation" is the imparting of knowledge, then "wisdom" has to do with the right use of this revelation in our lives day by day. The whole thrust of this request is for an enhanced knowledge of Father God and His ways. Therefore, it is of paramount importance that study of scripture is not regarded as a mere "duty", but that it is undertaken with the express purpose of acquiring a deeper understanding of the ways in which God is at work in our lives. Having received this revelation, there then must follow a desire to live out the truth that we have had revealed to us.

There is an urgent need for this truth to be taught in the church today. So many believers approach scripture simply in terms of study and a quest for knowledge. There is nothing wrong with this approach so long as it is accompanied with an earnest desire to "live out" what is being read. The Bible must never be relegated to the position of a mere text book, it is much more than that, it is food for the soul, and it provides the means through which we grow and become closer to Father God.

The Importance of Heart Knowledge

> *The eyes of your understanding being enlightened...*
>
> Ephesians 1:18 (N.K.J.V.)

> *I pray that the eyes of your heart may be enlightened...N.I.V*

> *I pray that your heart may be filled with light...*
>
> *New Living Translation*

Paul here is praying that our receiving of revelation may not just be on the basis of intellect, but that our hearts may be tender and therefore ready and willing to assimilate the truth we read. God desires to communicate with us at heart level so that our emotions are stirred to respond to all that He has procured for us. If we approach this simply as an exercise of the mind, we miss so much of what God desires to impart to us. This is why our emotions do have an important part to play in the pursuit of our walk with God. There are some who would argue that our emotions need to be suppressed and kept in control, but this flies in the face of all that Paul is praying in this majestic prayer. The greatness and the mercy of God, His boundless grace, and the manifestation of His love as seen in the giving of His son, the Lord Jesus Christ, must surely stir even the deepest of our emotions.

Why Heart Knowledge?

> ...That you may know what is the hope of His calling, what are the riches of the glory of His inheritance in the saints.
>
> Ephesians 1:18 (N.K.J.V.)

Paul, as he continues his prayer for the believers, prays to the Father for three things to be established in the hearts and minds of all saints:

The hope of His calling – the riches of the glory of His inheritance – the exceeding greatness of His power

Where there is a clear understanding of these great truths, victorious Christian living will be in evidence. So much we see by way of defeat and weakness is due to the fact that so many have failed to grasp the reality of what Paul is praying about here.

a) *The hope of His calling*

Paul here is praying with reference to the future destiny of the believer. He is affirming that this destiny is bound up within the framework of God's eternal purpose and has been decreed from before the foundation of the world. This truth needs to be clearly understood in the light of the warfare the believer engages in day by day. Whilst we rejoice in these magnificent "spiritual blessings" given us in Christ, we need to be ready to face the challenge presented by the powers of darkness. With this in mind, Paul is looking ahead to the day in which the church of Jesus Christ shall be displayed to the universe as Sons of God, and will reign with Him as His spotless bride. This is an aspect of our salvation which is future and to which we look forward with eager anticipation. It is the hope of our calling!

b) *The riches of the glory of His inheritance*

This statement takes us into the very depths of the relationship between Father God and the believer. We can look at this in two ways. We can observe the "saints" as being "His inheritance", in that God looks upon His children as a treasure beyond measure, "His own special people." This concept is borne out when we think in terms of the believer having been "bought with a price", the precious blood of Jesus Christ. This speaks of a massive investment of grace on God's part.

We can also look at this in terms of "inheritance" being expressed relative to the whole universe coming under the control of Jesus Christ, and the church, His bride, reigning with Him in glory.

Whichever way we look at it, we can see that Paul in his prayer is entering into a dimension that transcends our human reasoning, and only serves to establish the greatness and power of our God.

c) *The exceeding greatness of His power*

We live in a world in which the word "power" has so many meanings. We think for example in terms of political power, a power exercised by statesmen and governments both for good and for ill. There is military power as nations compete to possess the most advanced weaponry supposedly for defence purposes. There is economic power, seen in the workings of the great global institutions such as the World Bank and the International Monetary Fund. Then there is technological power as seen in recent decades as America and Russia locked horns in the so called "space race." Whilst the power of nations and of armies can be impressive, it pales into insignificance in comparison to the awesome power of God which he has manifested on behalf of the saints.

The scope of this power

> *It is the same mighty power that raised Christ from the dead and seated Him in the place of honour at God's right hand in the heavenly realms.*
>
> Ephesians 1:20 (New Living Translation)

To further describe the magnitude of this power, Paul in his prayer makes reference to the greatest manifestation of God's power ever seen, namely, the resurrection of His Son, the Lord Jesus Christ from the dead. This same power is at work in the procurement of our salvation and is the power that establishes our relationship with the Father.

As Jesus Christ hung upon the cross, Satan and all the forces at his disposal, sought to destroy Him once and for all, and thereby render the salvation of sinful man impossible. Christ's

221

resurrection was a shattering defeat for Satan and brought about the sentence of death upon him and his hoards of evil spirits. The salvation of the believer has been made possible through Christ's resurrection, and this awesome display of power in raising Him from the dead is the same power that is at work in and through believers.

The first of Paul's prayers recorded here in the Ephesian epistle comes to a climax as he affirms the exalted Christ as the One who is far above all rule and authority and above every name. This not only pertains to this present world, but also in the one to come and throughout all eternity. The passion in the heart of Paul in this first prayer is for the believer to be imbued with spiritual illumination. He has prayed for that Spirit of wisdom and revelation to be granted them as they begin to realise the enormity of the blessings that God has procured for them. These blessings cannot be entered into through human understanding, they can only be experienced through the enabling power of the Holy Spirit. It is the Holy Spirit who enables the believer to understand that "all things" have been put under His feet, and that He is the head of this glorious body the church.

Prayer – The Growth of the Believer
Ephesians 3

This passage in the third chapter of this mighty epistle gives us yet another glimpse into the prayer life of the Apostle Paul. Mention has already been made concerning his passionate concern for the church in that he diligently prays for believers on a daily basis. The prayer recorded in the first chapter sees the apostle praying for all believers; that God would grant them spiritual illumination. This second prayer shows Paul praying for believers to be endued with strength. Both prayers illustrate the fervent desire in the heart of Paul for the church to fulfil her mission, having a secure knowledge of her position in Christ, and of her strength that comes through the empowering of the Spirit. This second prayer is prayed in response to some of the most profound revelation given to Paul concerning the make up of the church, the Body of Christ.

Paul has written concerning the great "mystery" revealed to him by the grace of God, a "mystery" that had been hidden up until this present time, but was now being revealed through the ministry of Paul and the apostles.

The Mystery

> *That the gentiles should be fellow heirs, of the same body, and partakers of his promise in Christ through the gospel.*
>
> Ephesians 3:6 (N.K.J.V.)

In the second chapter of this epistle, Paul describes the position of the Gentiles prior to Christ's work upon the cross. They were without Christ, excluded from God's people Israel, and playing no part in the covenants of promise, totally devoid of hope, and without God in the world. Christ's death on the cross has served to reverse this division, and now the Gentiles, who were separated from God, have been brought near to Him by the shedding of Jesus' blood. This incredible transformation in their status from being in a position of spiritual death to a situation in which they are the recipients of the riches of God's grace, motivates Paul to pray that they will live in the power and victory of their elevation before God.

Paul's Motive in Praying

> *For this reason I bow my knees to the Father of*
> *our Lord Jesus Christ.*
>
> Ephesians 3:14 (N.K.J.V.)

Paul was not only rejoicing in their exalted position as Gentile believers, but he was also mindful of the great privilege that was his in being called to preach this great message of the gospel. He refers to himself as,

> *To me, who am less that the least of all the saints,*
> *this grace has been given, that I may preach*
> *among the gentiles the unsearchable riches of*
> *Christ.*
>
> Ephesians 3:8 (N.K.J.V.)

Paul was always mindful of the measure of grace extended to him at his conversion, he is therefore quite overwhelmed that God assigned him the task of taking this great message to the Gentiles. Not only is this "mystery" being declared to Jew and Gentile, but also to the principalities and powers in the heavenly realms. He refers to the role the church plays in the expediting of this awesome task.

As Paul ponders these remarkable facts, he can do no other than bow the knee before the "Father of our Lord Jesus Christ." He bows the knee in an act of great humility as he realises his own transformation and that of the Gentiles. He is overcome with great joy as he comes to a renewed understanding of the magnitude of God's grace. Having given the reason behind his prayer, Paul now proceeds to pray specifically on behalf of all the saints. We immediately notice the intense passion employed by the apostle as he prays. He is calling upon God to bless His people out of the abundance of His grace.

Prayer: the growth of the believer

> *...To be strengthened with might through His spirit in the inner man.*
> Ephesians 3:16 (N.K.J.V.)

> *I pray that from His glorious unlimited resources He will give you mighty inner strength through His Holy Spirit.*
> Ephesians 3:16 (New Living Translation)

Paul, in making this petition, is asking for the believer to be endued with spiritual power so as to enable he or she to live victorious lives in the midst of a crooked and perverse society. In praying this prayer, Paul clearly understands that this "being strengthened" is accomplished through the ministry of the Holy Spirit in the life of the believer. It is "God" who empowers through the Spirit thus enabling His people, the church to complete the task of mission He has called them to.

The work of the Holy Spirit here must not be thought of just in terms of extraordinary manifestation of God's presence, but also a strengthening process giving believers the capacity to reflect the glory of God in a fallen world. Paul is praying for this process of strengthening to be outworked in "the inner man." This refers to the "spiritual" part of our nature, or the heart, the seat of our emotions.

References abound in scripture concerning the importance of the heart. The human heart has the potential to be the fountain of all manner of evil and perversion. The prophet Jeremiah reminds us that the heart is "desperately wicked." With this in mind, Paul's prayer is for the heart to be the place where Christ dwells in response to the purifying work of the Holy Spirit. The thrust of Paul's prayer is for Christ to "indwell" or to "feel at home" in the hearts of His children. Not only this, but that He may have unfettered access to every part of the believer's personality and character.

Prayer
The Growth of the Believer – Security

The abiding passion in the heart of Paul is for the personal growth and development of every believer. He realises that this growth process will be enhanced as they are secure in their standing before Christ,

> ... that you, being rooted and grounded in love.
>> Ephesians 3:17 (N.K.J.V.)

> ... may your roots go down deep into the soil of God's marvelous love.
>> Ephesians 3:17 (New Living Translation)

Rooted and Grounded

Paul is using the illustration of the well rooted tree, the roots of which go down into the depths of the soil. As the roots are firmly embedded in the nutritious soil, so our lives by virtue of God's grace, are rooted in the depths of His love. If the word "rooted" comes from the world of botany, "grounded" is a term taken from the world of architecture.

Grounded

This gives the picture of a tall building the foundations of which are driven deep into the depths of the earth. Many of the tallest buildings in the world are built upon foundations that are almost equal to their height, this is particularly true in regions that are prone to earthquake activity. The depth of the foundations provide stability so as to withstand the threat of earth tremors. The language employed by Paul in this prayer paints a wonderful picture of the believer's security in Jesus.

Prayer
The growth of the Believer – Understanding

> *...may be able to comprehend with all the saints what is the width and length and depth and height.*
> Ephesians 3:18 (N.K.J.V.)

Here again we see the great heart of Paul and his concern for fellow believers. He prays passionately for their spiritual growth and that their relationship with God may deepen day by day. He is seeking to find an adequate way of expressing the sheer magnitude of God's love shown toward the individual saint, but also to the wider body; the church. He uses the term, "with all the saints", and he does so as a token of his desire that all believers come to an understanding of their security in Christ Jesus. Paul follows this by giving expression to the dimension of God's love toward His children. This love can never be measured, it is beyond the scope of human reason, but Paul seeks to at least establish some marker post by which the believer can begin to understand the vastness of this love.

a) *Width*

This refers to the scope of God's grace in encompassing both Jew and Gentile, and bringing them into the life of the church. It affirms Christ's work of reconciliation on the cross, and underpins the task given the church to take the gospel of the Kingdom to "all nations."

b) *Length*

Paul in his prayer is giving expression to the concept of eternity and the sure inheritance that is the portion of every saint. It also affirms the truth he wrote in the first chapter in terms of eternity past, in that the believer is; "chosen in Christ from before the foundation of the world."

c) *Depth*

An important part of our spiritual growth is the continual realisation of what God has saved us from. It is not that we should be constantly looking to the past. There has to be a moving forward in the grace and mercy of God. However, we do need to remind ourselves of the extent to which Christ came down in order to redeem broken humanity. Paul, in his epistle to the Philippians reminds us how Jesus in obtaining our salvation "made Himself of no reputation", He took upon Himself the form of a "bondservant", this is the lowest rank of slave. He then became "obedient to death, even the death of the cross."

d) *Height*

Paul has already made reference to the fact that the believer has been *"raised with Christ and made to sit in the heavenly places in Christ Jesus."*

The prayer of Paul here can be likened to the task of the master artist as he paints a magnificent picture using broad strokes of the brush. Paul, in his prayer, encapsulates in a few sentences the blessings conferred upon all who come to faith in the Lord Jesus Christ. The repentant sinner is plucked out of the darkness of sin and brought into the glorious light of the gospel of Christ.

Prayer
The Growth of the Believer – Loving

> To know the love of Christ which passes knowledge; that you may be filled with all the fullness of God.
>
> Ephesians 3:19 (N.K.J.V.)

We come now to the climax of this magnificent prayer prayed by Paul for all believers. His prayer is for God's people to experience His love as a reality in their daily lives. Paul in praying in this way is almost contradicting himself in that he is asking for believers to "know" this love, and yet at the same time he is saying that this love is so incredible, it is beyond the reach of human understanding. The love that Paul describes here is a love that can never be fully explained or comprehended. The human mind just simply cannot come to terms with the sheer scale of this love, it transcends any other dimension of love known to mankind.

The fact that we can "know" this love only serves to reinforce the magnitude of grace afforded the believer at the point of salvation. It is also an additional factor in our understanding of the security we have in Christ.

The final great request prayed by the apostle is for the believer to be *"filled with all the fullness of God."*

> *...Then you will be filled with the fullness of love*
> *and power that comes from God.*
> Ephesians 3:19 (New Living Translation)

We can never measure in volume the fullness of God. His resources are beyond the comprehension of mere men. However, this does not prevent the believer seeking to know more of Him. Far from being some remote figure confining Himself to the heavenly realm, He is a God who desires to indwell the believer filling him with all of the riches His grace affords.

Conclusion
The Growth of the Believer – Paul's Prayers

Both of the prayers prayed by Paul in this epistle to the Ephesians were penned for the sake of all saints. They reflect his fervent passion and love for God's people, and his zeal in taking this great message of the gospel to the nations. His prayer recorded in the first chapter, is a prayer for believers to be "spiritually illumined", and that they may be able to know Him in a deeper way.

His prayer in the third chapter is for believers to be "spiritually strengthened" through the enabling power of the Holy Spirit. Both prayers, although different in content, flow from a heart that desires to see every child of God going on into maturity and attaining all that God has purposed for them.

A Fitting Climax

> *Now to Him who is able to do exceedingly abundantly above all that we ask or think, according to the power that works in us, to Him be glory in the church by Christ Jesus to all generations, for ever and ever. Amen.*
>
> Ephesians 3:20-21 (N.K.J.V.)

The prayer concludes with the magnificent expression of praise and thanksgiving to God calling for the manifestation of His glory to be seen in and through the church.

Chapter 12

Prayer and Fasting

While planning the writing of this book, careful thought was given as to the subject matter that should be included. I have written to give a broad Biblical framework for prayer in its many and varied expressions. We have examined incidents from both the Old and New Testaments in which prayer has been seen to play a vital role in the transformation of nations, communities, churches and individuals. In defining in some measure a Biblical framework for prayer, there is the hope and indeed the expectancy that this material may help believers to realise afresh the potential power for change that prayer brings. With this in mind it was of paramount importance that a chapter on the subject of prayer and fasting be included to examine from scripture incidents in which prayer, offered in partnership with fasting, became the means through which the power of God was made known.

Before we examine incidents from scripture, it is important that we remind ourselves of the situation facing the church today particularly, in the West. Terms such as "post Christian" are now being widely used in describing the religious life of present day society. Britain, once considered to be a "Christian" country, a nation that sent missionaries to the four corners of the world, has now become increasingly "secular", and pressures are being brought to bear upon the church to view herself as part of a "multi-faith" culture. All of the "great religions" are afforded the same degree of respect and any overt declaration of the Christian gospel is now considered to be "politically incorrect" and offensive to other faiths. The great Christian festivals of Christmas and Easter are being stripped of their real significance so as to keep in step with this "multi-faith" agenda. This situation is so serious that many consider the days of freedom to preach the Christian gospel to be numbered.

This train of events must be a cause of great concern for the church in Britain and must surely act as a powerful rallying call to believers to come before God in fervent prayer. Not only should we be concerned over the conditions in the West, but we need also to be mindful of the circumstances that prevail in many parts of the world where the church is experiencing severe persecution, particularly in the nations that come under the banner of Islam. Believers are paying the ultimate price in the laying down of their lives simply because of their love for Jesus Christ and the message of the gospel. It is reckoned that more Christians have been martyred in the last thirty years than in the entire two thousand year history of the church of Jesus Christ. It is vital that sustained prayer be offered on behalf of those believers who live under such conditions. This great challenge to the church only serves to remind us of the words spoken by Jesus to His disciples,

> *These things I have spoken to you, that in me you*
> *might have peace. In the world you will have*

tribulation; but be of good cheer, for I have overcome the world.

John 16:33 (N.K.J.V.)

The same warning was given by the Apostle Paul as he reflected upon the persecution he endured at Antioch, Iconium, and Lystra,

Yes, all who desire to live Godly in Christ Jesus will suffer persecution.

2 Timothy 3:12 (N.K.J.V.)

Paul, in writing to the Ephesians, refers to the warfare of the believer not being a warfare conducted in terms of *"flesh and blood,"* but against *"Principalities and powers, against the rulers of the darkness of this world, against spiritual wickedness in the heavenly realms."*

Prayer and Fasting
The Response of the Church

Recognising that the warfare directed against the church is supernatural in origin, there has to be on the part of the church a response that engages on the same level. Very often the response has been based upon intellectual persuasion and reason and has been lacking in conviction. Paul illustrates the futility of this approach in his second epistle to the Corinthians,

For the weapons of our warfare are not carnal, but mighty in God for pulling down strongholds, casting down arguments and every high thing that exalts itself against the knowledge of God,

> *bringing every thought into captivity to the obedience of Christ.*
>
> 2 Corinthians 10:4-5 (N.K.J.V.)

Prayer and intercession when offered in partnership with fasting, remains one of the most potent weapons in the armoury of the believer and the corporate body of the local church. We have identified some of the forces arrayed against the church, we could list many more, but suffice it to say that there are seasons in which the discipline of fasting is called for both in the life of the individual believer and in the corporate fellowship of the saints. Jesus talked in terms of "when you fast" and not "if." Fasting was a prominent feature of the life of the early church with the apostles very often leading the way. Strategy for mission and evangelism was often implemented following periods of prayer and fasting.

As has been the practice in previous chapters of this book, we are going to examine instances recorded in scripture, both from the Old and New Testaments in which fasting played a major role in securing victory for the people of God.

Prayer and Fasting
Moses – Deuteronomy 9: 9,18

The book of Deuteronomy is made up of the words spoken by Moses to the Children of Israel just prior to their entry into the Promised Land. Deuteronomy literally means; "Second Law", and so we have Moses addressing the generation who had survived the forty years wandering in the wilderness. Moses reminds them of the mistakes of their fathers who, due to their rebellion, failed to inherit the land, and thereby wasted away in the wilderness. This new generation had to learn from past

236

mistakes and to ensure that at all times they walked in obedience to God's commands. God was setting out the land before them, it was for them to go up and possess it, and to be the generation that would live in the promise made to Abraham, Isaac and Jacob. So as to assist them, Moses reminds them of the commands given to him by God at Mount Sinai, and he urges them not to repeat the mistakes of their fathers. In order to reinforce this message, Moses reminds them of one such calamity.

The Golden Calf Incident

We dealt at length with this incident in the first chapter; "Prayer and Presence." God had called Moses to Mount Horeb, (Sinai), where He communed with him and established the covenant that God desired to make with His people. On that occasion Moses stayed on the mountain for forty days and forty nights during which time he maintained a fast,

> *When I went up into the mountain to receive the tablets of stone, the tablets of the covenant which the Lord made with you, then I stayed on the mountain forty days and forty nights. I neither ate bread nor drank water.*
>
> Deuteronomy 9:9 (N.K.J.V.)

Moses recounts to the people how the Lord gave him the two tablets of stone on which He had written all the words spoken to him. At the end of the forty day period, God instructed Moses to descend from the mountain and return to the people he had led out of Egypt.

Due to his prolonged absence, the people assumed that he had deserted them, and in an act of gross rebellion they made a "golden calf" and regarded it as the "god" that had brought them out of Egypt. This error was compounded by Aaron who demonstrated weakness in failing to warn the people of the consequences of their actions.

Such was God's anger at this act of rebellion He purposed to wipe them out, but that He would in no way hold Moses responsible for this debacle. Moses, in reminding this new generation of the failure of their fathers, recounts how that in his sorrow at their rank disobedience, he threw the two tablets of stone on which were written the law to the ground and broke them in pieces. This was not only Moses displaying anger at the sin of the people, but also great sorrow, and it prompted him to embark upon a second forty day fast,

> *And I fell down before the Lord, as at the first forty days and forty nights; I neither ate bread nor drank water, because of all your sin which you committed in doing wickedly in the sight of the Lord, to provoke him to anger.*
>
> Deuteronomy 9:18 (N.K.J.V.)

What Motivated Moses to Fast?

It was not simply the sin and rebellion of the people, although that was very serious, the heart of Moses was distressed at the thought of God disinheriting His people who He had redeemed by His greatness and by His mighty hand. Such a decision would reflect badly upon God and would give the impression to the surrounding nations that He was unable to keep His covenant promised to Abraham, Isaac and Jacob. Moses is reminding this new generation of these calamitous events.

God's Response

The Lord God heeded the cry of Moses as he pleaded on behalf of the people and as he engaged in a second forty day fast. Although God regarded the people as a rebellious and a stubborn people, He nevertheless had mercy upon them, and responded to the prayer and fasting undertaken by Moses on their behalf.

Moses, here in the book of Deuteronomy, is drawing their attention to these failures and urging them not to repeat the same mistakes when they enter the Promised Land.

A Solemn Reminder

> *Remember! Do not forget how you provoked the Lord your God to wrath in the wilderness. From the day you departed from the land of Egypt until you came to this place, you have been rebellious against the Lord.*
>
> Deuteronomy 9:7 (N.K.J.V.)

Only the intercessory prayer and the fasting of Moses saved the people from total destruction.

Prayer and Fasting
Samuel – 1 Samuel 7

Here we have another situation in which disaster was averted through the prayer and fasting of a company of people. It is helpful to know something of the background to this story and the intervention of Samuel. The nation of Israel had been descending into a moral and spiritual abyss through the weak leadership of Eli, and the blatant sin of his two sons, Hophni and Phineas.

Things came to a head resulting in the nation being attacked by the Philistines, and the Ark of the Covenant being captured. Such was the distress caused in the wake of this catastrophe, Eli fell over backwards and died upon hearing of Israel's defeat, the capture of the Ark, and the death of his two sons. The wife of Phineas, the daughter-in-law of Eli, was about to give birth. When she heard of the defeat and the news of the death of her husband and also the capture of the Ark, she died in childbirth. She gave birth to a son which she called, *"Ichabod"* which means *"The glory of the Lord has departed."* Following these dreadful events, the nation of Israel descended into a spiritual morass and lived in constant fear of the Philistines.

For the Philistines, the capture of the Ark proved to be an act that had disastrous consequences for their people. The Ark, immediately upon capture, was placed in the temple of the Philistine god, Dagon. The following morning Dagon was found upon his face, smashed in pieces. As an act of severe judgement upon the Philistines, the Lord afflicted the land with a plague that manifested itself in the form of tumours. The plague hit many parts of the territory of the Philistines and was thought by many to be the bubonic plague, in that reference is made in the narrative to the presence of rats.

Such was the distress of the Philistines, they took steps to return the Ark to Israel, to its rightful location. The plague had inflicted great suffering and destruction upon the Philistines and so the Ark was returned accompanied with a "trespass offering." This offering took the form of five golden tumours, and five golden rats.

The Ark eventually comes into the possession of the men of Kirjath-Jeraim, and was brought into the house of Abinadab, where it remained for twenty years. The return of the Ark was followed by a season of national repentance as Samuel led the people in an act of contrition before God. The people earnestly sought for deliverance from the constant threat of the Philistines, but they could only receive help from God by forsaking all heathen idols and religious idolatries,

...If you return to the Lord with all your hearts, then put away the foreign gods and the images of Canaanite goddesses from among you, and prepare your heart for the Lord, and serve Him only; and He will deliver you from the hand of the Philistines.

1 Samuel 7:3 (N.K.J.V.)

It is interesting to note how putting away foreign gods became the key to national renewal. There is a powerful lesson for the church to take on board here as she seeks to engage in the battle for the souls of men and women and young people. Individual believers and indeed the corporate body of the local church will fail in this battle if there is the presence of "idols" that grieve the Holy Spirit and thereby reduce spiritual power.

The children of Israel responded to the call of Samuel and took steps to destroy all traces of Baal worship including altars, poles and other forbidden items. When Samuel saw that the people were responding to his message, he called all Israel together at Mizpah. He prayed to God on their behalf while the people fasted.

Prayer and Fasting

So they gathered together at Mizpah, drew water, and poured it out before the Lord. And they fasted

*that day, and said there, we have sinned against
the Lord...*

1 Samuel 7:6 (N.K.J.V.)

God's Response
Victory over their Enemies

When the Philistines heard that Israel had gathered at Mizpah, they mounted an attack expecting a rapid victory. When this became known to the children of Israel, they were initially overcome with fear and cried to God for Him to intervene,

> *...Do not cease to cry out to the Lord our God for us, that he may save us from the hand of the Philistines.*

1 Samuel 7:8 (N.K.J.V.)

Samuel came before the Lord and brought a whole burnt offering on behalf of the nation crying out to the God of Israel, and the Lord heard him. As Samuel was making the burnt offering, the Lord "thundered" upon the Philistines causing them to be overcome with confusion. All the men of Israel then pursued the Philistines and drove them back as far as Beth Car,

> *So the Philistines were subdued, and they did not come any more into the territory of Israel. And the hand of the Lord was against the Philistines all the days of Samuel. Then the cities which the Philistines had taken from Israel were restored to Israel. From Ekron to Gath; and Israel recovered its territory from the hands of the Philistines...*

1 Samuel 7:13-14 (N.K.J.V.)

From a situation in which the nation of Israel was dispossessed of her territories, locked into the worship of pagan gods, and always at the mercy of a powerful enemy, she now found herself reconciled to God, lost territories restored, and the Philistine threat removed.

All of this was brought about by the power of prayer and fasting entered into under the strong leadership of Samuel. This season of prayer and fasting was a clear indication before God that the people were truly sorry for their sin, and were committed to following Him in faith and obedience.

Praying for a Nation

There are clear principles for the church to learn from this story as she seeks to respond to the challenge of the hour.

Prayer and Fasting
Ezra

The events recorded in the book of Ezra have to do with the aftermath of the demise of the Babylonian empire and the return of the exiles to the land of Judah. The nation of Judah had been destroyed by the armies of Babylon, and thousands had been carried away into captivity, a period that was to last for seventy years.

This process began with the decree given by Cyrus the Mede to rebuild the temple at Jerusalem which had been totally destroyed by the armies of Nebuchadnezzar. This decree was followed by the first expedition of returning exiles under the leadership of Zerubbabel. The foundation of the temple was built, but a wave of persecution, coupled by a loss of vision on the part of the returned exiles, resulted in a sixteen year period in which all work came to a halt. The eventual completion of the task was undertaken in response to the visionary ministries of the two prophets, Haggai and Zechariah.

The second company of returning exiles left Babylon in 458 BC under the leadership of Ezra who was to assume a position of spiritual leadership over the people. It was through the leadership of Ezra that a much needed wave of renewal began to touch the nation, a renewal that brought in its wake radical reform.

The Returning Exiles
Ezra 8

The first part of chapter eight gives us a comprehensive list of all who returned to Judah as part of Ezra's company. Ezra arranged a meeting point at which all who intended to go on this journey would meet. This was to be a potentially hazardous exercise not only in terms of the dangerous terrain, but also in terms of security. The returning exiles would be taking with them many items of gold and silver that had been confiscated from the temple by the Babylonian armies, but were now being returned. Ezra was fully aware of the risk factor in undertaking this journey, but his trust and confidence was in God. He called the people together to pray before embarking on this hazardous route,

> *Then I proclaimed a fast there on the river of Ahava, that we might humble ourselves before our God, to seek from Him the right way for us and our little ones and all our possessions.*
>
> Ezra 8:21 (N.K.J.V.)

This verse, quite apart from the context in which it is set, teaches us some very powerful lessons concerning the correct motive for entering into a season of fasting. Ezra realised the enormity of the moment, and for him it was essential for there to be a "humbling before God!" So very often people approach fasting as an exercise merely to secure some provision from God, often in the midst of a crisis situation. There may be times and seasons in which this approach may be legitimate, but there is the risk of questionable motive.

Isaiah warned against wrong motives in relation to fasting. God instructed him to warn the people concerning their improper motives when engaging in this discipline. In Isaiah's day, fasting had degenerated into a mere display of religious pride very similar to that of the Pharisees in the period of Christ's ministry. In spite of their repeated seasons of fasting, frustration abounded in that it seemed that God was not responding to their efforts,

> *We have fasted before you they say. Why aren't you impressed? We have done much penance, and you don't even notice it.*
> Isaiah 58:3 (New Living Translation)

God responds to their complaint through the ministry of the prophet Isaiah and rebukes them for their religious charade. Their periods of fasting were accompanied by infighting, quarrelling and the continued exploitation of those who worked for them. God saw through it all and condemned them for their injustice and mistreatment of the poor.

The Fasting God Honours

> *No, the kind of fasting I want calls you to free those who are wrongly imprisoned and to stop*

> *oppressing those who work for you. Treat them*
> *fairly and give them what they earn.*
>
> Isaiah 58:6 (New Living Translation)

The approach of the people in Isaiah's day was in marked contrast to the attitude called for by Ezra. He called for the people to humble themselves before God, and to seek from Him the right way. Prayer and fasting must always be viewed as an exercise in humbling ourselves before God as we come before Him in complete surrender.

Prayer for Protection

Ezra was mindful of the risks involved in an expedition of this nature. Not only was he responsible for the personal safety of all who travelled with him, but there was also the added responsibility of securing the items of gold and silver that were to be returned for temple worship in Jerusalem. Whilst recognising the danger ahead, Ezra did not want to have to approach the king requesting an escort of soldiers and horsemen. Ezra sought to place his full trust and confidence in the protecting power of God alone, and not to seek the services of the king.

Prayer and Fasting

> *So we fasted and entreated our God for this, and*
> *He answered our prayer.*
>
> Ezra 8:23 (N.K.J.V.)

Ezra and the returning exiles arrived in Jerusalem and the articles of gold and silver for the temple were safely delivered.

Prayer and Fasting
Old Testament

There are many references to fasting in the Old Testament. For example, Daniel, following his research concerning the times and seasons of the Babylonian captivity, falls before God as he understands the implication for God's people of the statement made by Jeremiah, namely, that this period of captivity would last for seventy years,

> *Then I set my face toward the Lord God to make request and supplications, with fasting, sackcloth, and ashes.*
>
> Daniel 9:3 (N.K.J.V.)

Daniel prays a prayer of vicarious repentance on behalf of the people of God who, in spite of the many warnings given them by a succession of prophets, failed to take heed, and found themselves in captivity at the hand of the Babylonians. Daniel, in realising the enormity of their sin, humbles himself before God on their behalf.

This powerful prayer of repentance, prayed in the context of a fast, is followed by a powerful revelation of the purposes of God concerning the future of the nation of Israel and Jerusalem in particular. In Daniel's experience, fasting became the vehicle through which he was able to understand the mind and will of God concerning events ranging from the immediate, right up to and including the coming of the Lord Jesus Christ to establish His permanent Kingdom.

Prayer and Fasting
Jonah

Following Jonah's initial reluctance to preach in Ninevah and his subsequent encounter with the great fish, Jonah eventually reaches the great city and delivers God's message to the inhabitants,

> *...Yet forty days and Ninevah shall be overthrown.*
>
> Jonah 3:4 (N.K.J.V.)

> *So the people of Ninevah believed God, proclaimed a fast, and put on sackcloth, from the greatest to the least of them.*
>
> Jonah 3:5 (N.K.J.V.)

Led by the king, the whole city came before God in fasting and in an act of great humility as the people recognised God for who He was, and gave heed to the message of Jonah,

> *Then God saw their works, that they turned from their evil way; and God relented from the disaster that He said He would bring upon them, and He did not do it.*
>
> Jonah 3:10 (N.K.J.V.)

There are many more references to fasting in the Old Testament that would merit our attention, but we are now going to take this a stage further by looking at some of the examples of prayer and fasting recorded in the New Testament. We shall see how fasting brought about dramatic change in the circumstances of both individuals and corporate groups of people.

Reference has already been made to the teaching of Jesus in respect of fasting. He used the terminology, "When you fast." He not only "taught" fasting, but on a number of occasions He clearly demonstrated the potential power that can be released as believers engage on this level. He also gave clear instructions as to the way fasting should be approached. Matthew records Jesus words as part of His "Sermon on the Mount", and in particular His teaching of charitable deeds, prayer, and fasting. He warns against the danger of being seen to do these acts in public as a display of religious pride and hypocrisy. Jesus was seeking to expose the flawed motives of the Pharisees who always sought an audience when engaging in their religious observance. Such conduct incurred the wrath of Jesus and prompted Him to issue severe warnings,

> *Moreover, when you fast, do not be like the hypocrites, with a sad countenance. For they disfigure their faces that they may appear to men to be fasting. Assuredly, I say to you, they have their reward.*
>
> Matthew 6:16 (N.K.J.V.)

Having exposed the false motives of the Pharisees in respect to fasting, Jesus then proceeds to teach the correct way in which it should be approached,

> *But you when you fast, comb your hair and wash your face. Then no one will suspect you are fasting, except your Father, who knows what you do in secret. And your Father, who knows all secrets, will reward you.*
>
> Matthew 16:17-18 (New Living Translation)

There may be occasions in which it may be legitimate for us to share with a fellow believer that we are fasting in response to the prompting of the Holy Spirit. There will also be situations in which a local assembly of believers may participate in seasons of fasting when invited to by Spirit filled leadership. The teaching of Jesus here in Matthew's gospel is designed to protect believers from the danger of wrong motives when considering this vital ministry of fasting.

Having established these important guidelines, we now go on to examine instances in the life and ministry of Jesus in which fasting played a vital role.

His temptations
Luke 4

Here we have Jesus just about to commence His earthly ministry having experienced the enduement of the Holy Spirit at the Jordan. Luke records how Jesus, following His baptism, returns to Jordan in the power of the Spirit and was led by the Spirit into the wilderness. There follows a dramatic encounter with Satan in which he seeks to sabotage the ministry of Jesus before it even started. Fasting became an absolute necessity for Jesus as He prepared Himself for this encounter,

> *Being tempted for forty days by the devil. And in those days He ate nothing, and afterward, when they had ended, He was hungry.*
>
> Luke 4:2 (N.K.J.V.)

Matthew, Mark and Luke describe in vivid detail this dramatic encounter between Jesus and the devil. Knowing that Jesus was hungry, the devil invited Him to command the stones to become bread. He prefaced this invitation with the caustic remark; *"If you are the Son of God?"* He then took Jesus onto the peak of a high mountain showing Him all the kingdoms of the world in a moment of time and inviting Jesus to worship him. He then brought Jesus to Jerusalem and set Him on the pinnacle of the temple, inviting Him to throw Himself down on the basis of the scripture that promised protection in the event of dashing one's foot on a stone. Jesus refuted each one of these temptations by quoting scripture, "It is written." Satan, realising the failure of his mission, departs from Jesus for a season.

The Outcome in Relation to Fasting

> *Jesus returned in the power of the Spirit to Galilee, and news of Him went throughout all the surrounding region. And He taught in their synagogues, being glorified by all.*
> Luke 4:14-15 (N.K.J.V.)

Following this, Jesus came into Nazareth, and as was His custom, He went into the synagogue and stood up to read. He used the occasion to define the nature and purpose of His mission and the authority in which He would operate. His ministry was to be a ministry conducted through the empowering of the Holy Sprit, and His message would be directed to the poor, the broken-hearted, the oppressed, and those who found themselves marginalized from everyday society.

Prayer and Fasting
Confronting Demonic Power

The gospel writers vividly record how Jesus came to preach the gospel of the Kingdom of God. At the heart of His message was the need for "repentance" and a turning away from sin, this was foundational to entry into the Kingdom. His ministry was also characterised by the manifestation of supernatural power as shown in His many miracles of healing, the raising of the dead and the deliverance of those oppressed by demonic power. Reference has been made in previous chapters of this book concerning the ministry of Jesus and the early church; ministries performed in and through the power of the Holy Spirit.

The incident recorded here by Mark illustrates the clear link that exists between fasting and the manifestation of Kingdom power.

The Mount of Transfiguration
Mark 9

The story begins with Jesus taking Peter, James and John up onto a high mountain. Suddenly the appearance of Jesus changed in that He was transformed into a figure that became dazzling white, whiteness well beyond the scope of any launderer to reproduce. In addition to this, the disciples saw Moses and Elijah standing talking to Jesus. Peter was so overcome by this experience he suggested that three tabernacles be built; one for Jesus, one for Moses, and one for Elijah. The disciples were overcome with fear as a cloud enveloped them, and as a voice sounded from the cloud, saying,

> *This is my beloved Son, hear Him!*
> Mark 9:7 (N.K.J.V.)

Suddenly they looked and found themselves to be alone with Jesus. Jesus warned the three disciples that they were not to relate this incident to any other person.

Jesus and the three disciples descend from the mountain to the valley below where they are confronted with a crowd who were in a state of agitation over the failure of the disciples to cast a demon out of a young boy brought to them by his father.

From the Mountain to the Valley

The father of the boy comes before Jesus in a state of great distress over the desperate condition of his demonised boy,

> *And wherever it siezes him, it throws him down; he foams in the mouth, gnashes his teeth, and becomes rigid. So I spoke to your disciples that they should cast it out, but they could not.*
>
> Mark 9:18 (N.K.J.V.)

The failure on the part of the disciples to cast the evil spirit out of the poor boy incurred the displeasure of Jesus,

> *...O unbelieving generation, how long shall I be with you? How long shall I bear with you? Bring him to me.*
>
> Mark 9:19 (N.K.J.V.)

Jesus in using the term, *"faithless generation"* was not only referring to the failure of the disciples in ministering to the boy, but also to the onlookers, all of whom were part of the unbelieving generation that Jesus so often confronted during His ministry. Jesus then responds to the heart cry of the father as he pleads before Him on behalf of his demented son.

The Response of Jesus

> ...If you can believe, all things are possible to him who believes.
>
> Mark 9:23 (N.K.J.V.)

The father immediately cries out in response to these words spoken by Jesus, *"Lord I believe; help my unbelief."*

Jesus then turned His attention to the demonised boy and commanded the deaf and dumb spirit to leave him. The evil spirit cried out and threw the boy into another violent convulsion before being expelled at the command of Jesus.

The boy lay motionless as if dead, but Jesus took him by the hand and lifted him up. The boy got up, totally delivered from the grip of evil spirits.

Following this, Jesus and His disciples enter a house where they enquire of Him the reason behind their failure in casting the demon out of the boy,

> So He said to them, *"This kind can come out by nothing but prayer and fasting."*
>
> Mark 9:29 (N.K.J.V.)

The disciples had encountered the presence of evil spirits on previous occasions and had often seen positive results, but this incident was possibly the most severe case they had ever encountered.

The important word we need to examine here is the word, "kind." In the Greek, this word refers to, "family, race, kindred, or generation," and it is this type of demonic presence that requires the discipline of fasting in order for freedom to be granted the victim.

Given the unprecedented rise in the activity of the occult in our society today, this statement of Jesus concerning the necessity of fasting is a clear directive to the church as she seeks to minister into these very difficult situations.

Prayer and Fasting
The Early Church

The power of the Holy Spirit came upon the disciples on the Day of Pentecost enabling them to preach the gospel of the Kingdom with the same power and authority demonstrated by Jesus during His ministry. From Pentecost onwards the mission of the church expanded in response to the tide of persecution following the death of Stephen. Many of the early believers were "scattered abroad", and went everywhere preaching Jesus. Political, cultural, and racial boundaries were crossed as the Gentiles also received the gospel and experienced the mighty dynamic of the Holy Spirit. A thriving church was established in Antioch which became the base from which Paul and Barnabas were released into mission.

The events surrounding Paul and Barnabas are covered in chapter ten of this book, but it is important to understand the part that prayer and fasting played in the birthing of their mission. Following a period of ministry in Antioch, the Apostles took the gospel to Iconium where they preached with great power, the Lord confirming their word with mighty signs and wonders. From

Iconium, they came to Lystra and Derbe, cities of Lyconia, where they preached the gospel again with the manifestation of healing power. When they came to Lystra they witnessed one of the most dramatic miracles recorded in the book of Acts. They encountered a man who was a cripple, and had been in that condition since birth. Luke records how this poor man listened intently as Paul preached. Paul, preaching under the powerful anointing of the Holy Spirit, saw the man and perceived that he possessed a faith that he would be healed,

> *Paul said with a loud voice, stand up straight upon your feet! And he leaped and walked.*
> Acts 14:10 (N.K.J.V.)

There followed amazing scenes as the onlookers surged forward thinking that Paul and Barnabas were gods. Opposition quickly followed resulting in Paul being stoned and left for dead. His followers lifted him up and led him back into the city and from there they returned to Lystra, Iconium, and Antioch.

Prayer and Fasting
The Local Church

> *So when they had appointed elders in every church, and prayed with fasting, they commended them to the Lord in whom they had believed.*
> Acts 14:10 (N.K.J.V.)

This illustrates the passion Paul had for the life and witness of the local church. In establishing a local witness, Paul laid the twin foundation of prayer and fasting. The story began with the praying and fasting of the Antioch church, Paul was anxious for this pattern to continue.

Prayer and fasting
The Example set by Paul

The ministry of Paul had a powerful impact upon the life of the early church, but it must always be borne in mind that this ministry was exercised at great personal cost to the apostle.

On numerous occasions there were those who questioned his credibility as an apostle, many of his detractors dismissed him as a fraud. In his second letter to the church at Corinth, Paul bears his soul as he responds to the malicious attacks made upon him by those who opposed him. Fasting is clearly seen as a powerful weapon in his armoury,

> *In stripes, in imprisonments, in tumults, in labours, in sleeplessness, in fastings.*
> 2 Corinthians 6:5 (N.K.J.V.)

Paul lists the dangers he endured for the gospel including imprisonment, beatings, being attacked by robbers, perils at sea, weariness,

> *In toil, in sleeplessness, in hunger and thirst, in fastings, often, in cold and nakedness.*
> 2 Corinthians 11:27 (N.K.J.V.)

In addition to these physical deprivations, Paul bore the daily burden of the churches and their spiritual health. Paul may have had a ministry of awesome power, but there was a very great cost involved. This is something that must be taken into account by all who seek to enter into ministry and service.

Conclusion

Mention has already been made concerning the great challenge facing the church of Jesus Christ in our present day. One of the major problems is the failure on the part of believers, and this must include leaders, to fully come to terms with the moral and spiritual vacuum that is systemic in western society. So very often there is either a malaise as God's people fail to engage in recognising the threat of the enemy, but there is the other danger and that is "cheap triumphalism," the celebration of a victory for which the battle has not yet been fought!

Where the testimony of the church is making dramatic inroads is in situations in which prayer and fasting are seen to be the absolute essential ingredients in seeing the work of the Kingdom progress. There are no short cuts to be taken when seeking national and community transformation, the price has to be paid! Let us resolve to be part of the great prayer army that God is building from every nation and embracing every stream and tradition. God will always respond to the cry of His people,

> *If my people who are called by my name will humble themselves, and pray and seek my face, and turn from their wicked ways, then I will hear from heaven, and will forgive them their sin and heal their land.*
>
> 2 Chronicles 7:14 (N.K.J.V.)H

Author's profile

Alistair Cole: As Chairman of the National Prayer Network of the Elim Pentecostal Churches he is responsible for co-ordinating prayer strategy for the Elim churches. He is a regular speaker at national, regional and local prayer conferences.

Commendations

"The greatest fringe benefit of being a Christian is prayer. This book will inspire you to engage in prayer more than ever."

Rev. Dr. R T Kendall: International Bible Teacher.
Former Minister; Westminster Chapel, London.

"This excellent book not only challenges the reader to encounter God in the place of prayer but gives a Biblical basis on which answers can be expected. I believe it to be a tool that should be at the disposal of every Christian who is serious about creating spiritual change through persistent intercession."

Rev. John Glass: General Superintendent
Elim Pentecostal Churches.

"Alistair Cole sets out an excellent biblical and practical framework for prayer. It is an inspiring and helpful work and will be a blessing for all those who want a solid foundation for their prayer life."

Rev. Colin Dye: Senior Minister, Kensington Temple, London, Apostolic Leader; London City Church.

"This book gives an excellent overview of prayer in both the Old and New Testaments. I highly recommend it."

Rev. Lyndon Bowring:

Executive Chairman, CARE, Chancellor of Regents Theological College.

"This is a timely book which brings us back to the foundations of what the Bible really says about prayer and it will encourage and equip us to go on praying with renewed faith."

Jane Holloway: National Prayer Director, World Prayer Centre, Birmingham, England, Hope 08 National Leadership Team.
